The Civil War:
The War Between the States

Authors: George Lee and Roger Gaston
Consultants: Schyrlet Cameron and Suzanne Myers
Editor: Mary Dieterich
Proofreader: Margaret Brown

COPYRIGHT © 2018 Mark Twain Media, Inc.

ISBN 978-1-62223-690-9

Printing No. CD-405013

Mark Twain Media, Inc., Publishers
Distributed by Carson-Dellosa Publishing LLC

The purchase of this book entitles the buyer to reproduce the student pages for classroom use only. Other permissions may be obtained by writing Mark Twain Media, Inc., Publishers.

All rights reserved. Printed in the United States of America.

Visit us at www.carsondellosa.com

Table of Contents

Introduction

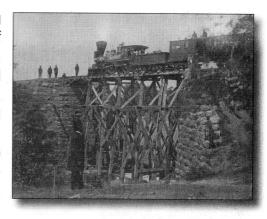

The Civil War was the major dividing point separating America's youth from its adulthood. The central figures of this epic event are still larger than life: Lincoln, Lee, Jackson, and Grant. Each year thousands of Americans go to Civil War battlefields, debate the war in Civil War Roundtables, perform reenactments, and write and buy books and magazines concerning this four-year period in our history. It was a very complicated war, and your students need to understand what happened and why. This book is not an in-depth study of the war; it is for students who need to learn the basic story as accurately as possible.

This book is intended to do more than tell about battles, however. We have also included information about how the struggle began, what Congress was doing, how the war affected slavery, and information about weapons and army organization.

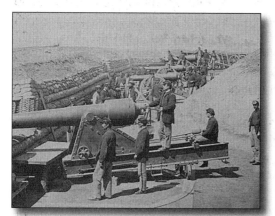

For many students, the Civil War is one of the most fascinating periods in American history. Hopefully, the lessons in this book will help the war come alive. Students will be able to imagine the cannons of Gettysburg booming, Jackson on the loose in the Shenandoah Valley, Lincoln trying to find a general who knows how to win, and Robert E. Lee becoming the most admired (or feared) military man since George Washington.

Remind students that many young men, some 12 and 13, were in uniform as drummers. Their sisters were working with the women in preparing bandages and worrying about their fathers, brothers, and uncles who were facing death or injury on the battlefield that very day. Students need to realize that decisions were being made and debated each day. Use class discussions to involve students in those debates in order to reinforce student learning concerning the people making the decisions during the Civil War. Use students' enthusiasm to foster interest in other historical studies. What they learn about the past may help them make better decisions in the future.

Each of the 43 lessons contained in the book *The Civil War* includes a reading selection followed by an activity skills page. Teachers may choose to combine several lessons into a unit of study. The lessons are designed as stand-alone material for the classroom or home schooling setting. Also, the book can be used as supplemental material to enhance the social studies curriculum in the classroom, for independent study, or as a tutorial at home.

—The Authors

States' Rights and Slavery

The writers of the Constitution had done many things well, and for that wisdom they deserved the tribute of their nation. But a serious question had not been answered. Was this a union formed by the PEOPLE of the United States, or by the people of the United STATES? To us, this seems a trivial question, but it was one debated endlessly in the early days of the republic.

Doctrine of Nullification

James Madison, in opposing the Sedition Act in 1799, said that states had the right to nullify (cancel) unauthorized actions by Congress. New Englanders favored this position at the Hartford Convention during the War of 1812, and John C. Calhoun of South Carolina later developed that theory into a doctrine accepted by most Southerners. Simply put, the doctrine stated if Congress went too far, a state had the right to prevent a law from being enforced inside its boundaries.

Daniel Webster, during a debate with Robert Hayne in 1830, said that if there is a problem with either the Constitution or the way it is being applied, the solution is to amend it. The Union had been good for the country in every way, he said, and as long as it existed, the future was bright. He closed with the famous words: "Liberty and Union, now and forever, one and inseparable!" But by 1860, more than words were needed to settle the debate.

Slavery

The United States were held together by a fragile cord by the 1850s. The differences were not just in what people said, but in the way they thought. The South preferred tradition; the North was excited by change. The South valued land, while the North found prosperity in business and trade. The South used slave labor, while the North used low-paid immigrants to do the hardest jobs in factories. The South gave power to aristocrats called planters; the North was governed by middle-class politicians.

The first time slavery became a big issue was in 1820 as Congress debated whether it should admit Missouri as a slave state. A compromise was fashioned by Henry Clay, allowing Missourians to keep slavery if they chose. Those territories of the Louisiana Purchase south of 36° 30' would be open to slavery; territories north of that line would be closed to slavery. During debate, a few northern Congressmen called slavery a "sin," and their tone alarmed Thomas Jefferson. In a letter to John Holmes about the Compromise, he wrote ". . . this momentous question, like a fire bell in the night, awakened and filled me with terror. I considered it at once as the [death] knell of the Union." The Missouri Compromise was accepted, and attention turned to less heated topics.

A solution to slavery that was popular at the time was colonization—a movement to send free black people to Africa, or find an isolated place for them in Central America. Many white leaders liked this idea, and in 1822, a colony was established on a piece of African coastline that they named Liberia. However, northern blacks were opposed to colonizing; they considered themselves American. Others, called abolitionists, opposed both colonizing and slavery. Their most well-known spokesman, William Lloyd Garrison, began his newspaper, *The Liberator,* in 1831. From then on, the fire-bell rang often.

Activity: Primary Source
Go online to <https://www.loc.gov/exhibits/jefferson/159.html> to read a transcript of the letter sent from Thomas Jefferson to John Holmes discussing his opinion of the Missouri Compromise.

Name: _____ Date: _____

Activity: Recalling Information

Directions: Use information from the reading selection to answer the questions.

1. What was the doctrine of nullification?

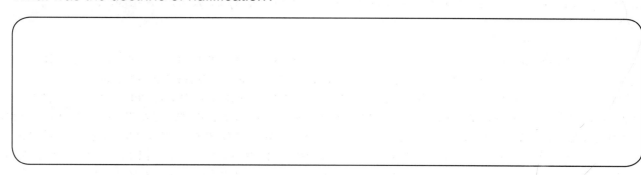

2. What was the Colonization Movement?

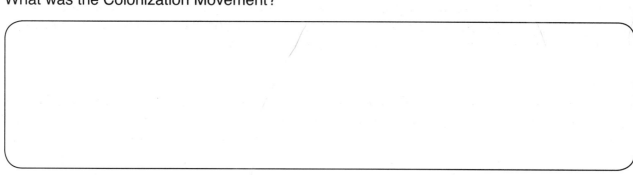

3. By the 1850s, what were the differences between the North and the South?

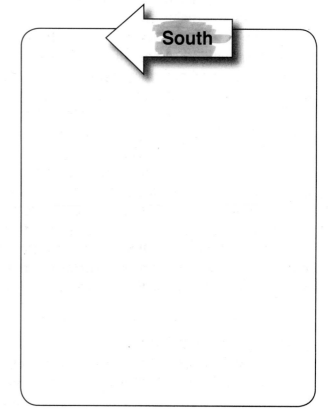

The South Before the War

If you look at a map of the United States in 1860, you may notice that the area of slave states looks larger than that of the free states. The South covered 896,000 square miles, and the North (excluding distant Oregon and California) only 557,000 square miles. Between 1820 and 1860, the South's population grew, but not as rapidly as the North's. This fact bothered Southerners because northern states would get larger majorities in the House of Representatives. After Nat Turner's slave rebellion in 1831, and with fear growing that abolitionists would stir up more trouble in the future, Southerners saw trouble ahead.

This map from 1860 shows slave states in the darkest shade, free states in a slightly lighter shade, and the territories in the lightest shade. Slavery would be allowed in most of the territories if the people voted for it.

Southern whites were not all alike, however. Extending all the way from Maryland and Delaware to Texas, the South's geography was a mixture of mountains and fertile valleys, forests and plains. The crops varied from one region to the next. Tobacco was the main crop of Maryland, Kentucky, and Virginia; hemp and corn in Missouri; sugar in Louisiana; and rice in the South Carolina lowlands. However, the crop that most represented the South was cotton.

Economic Hierarchy

In economic status and influence, there were great differences. At the top of Southern society were the planters, owners of more than 20 slaves. The 1860 census included only 46,274 planters; less than 3,000 owned 100 or more slaves; only 11 held 500 or more slaves. The size of a plantation was limited by the time it took for a slave to reach the most distant fields, so a planter might own several plantations. In numbers they were few, but in economic and political influence the planters were powerful. Some lived in great mansions, but most preferred reinvesting their wealth in more land, horses, and slaves.

The merchant and professional class also had influence. Many of them also owned slaves, and some dreamed of the day when they would become planters. The largest customer of the merchant or lawyer and the largest contributor to the church was the planter; so, the attorney, merchant, and minister were all tied to the slave system. Small plantation owners or farmers with fewer than 20 slaves often had more invested in slaves than in horses and mules. This gave them a reason to want to continue the slave system.

At the bottom of white society were poor white people. Often, they were illiterate and isolated. However, their pride would not permit them to do the work of slaves. While not all poor whites fit this stereotype, they were definitely a class of people looked down upon by others. Richer people did not ridicule them (the men could vote); they just ignored them.

Among the black population in the South, there were two groups: free and slave. In 1860, less than 10% of blacks in the South were free. The majority of free blacks lived in cities where it was easier to find work. Slaves were at the bottom of Southern society. Slave labor was used for labor-intensive agricultural products: cotton, tobacco, and sugar. Sometimes, planters hired out their slaves to other planters or tradesmen.

Name: _____ Date: _____

Activity: Key Details

Directions: Use information in the reading selection to complete the graphic organizer.

Economic Hierarchy in the South

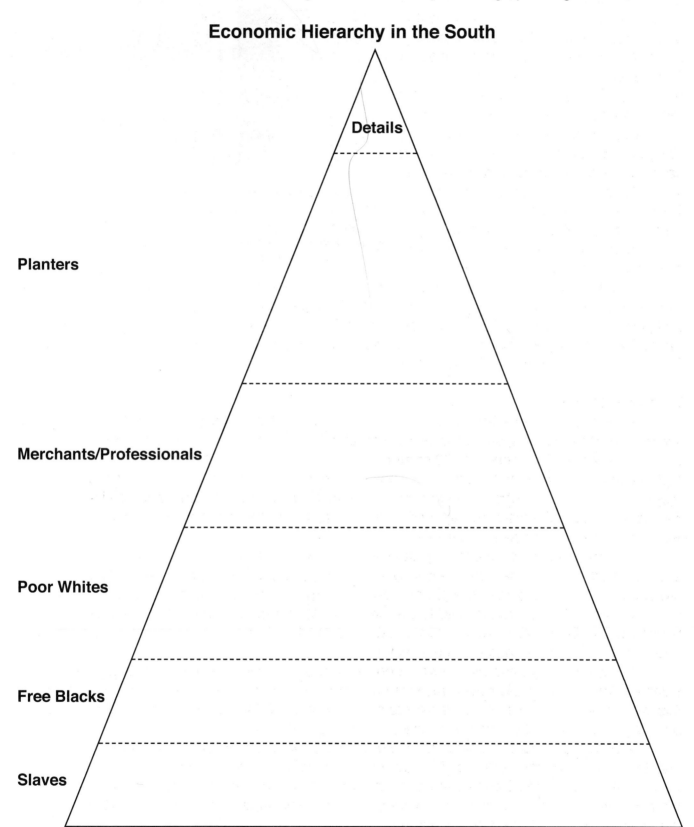

Planters

Merchants/Professionals

Poor Whites

Free Blacks

Slaves

Details

The North Before the War

Locomotives were rapidly replacing steamboats in the pre-war North.

As one crossed the Mason-Dixon Line between Pennsylvania and Maryland, or traveled down the Ohio River on a steamboat, he found himself between two different worlds. The difference came from technology, transportation and communications networks, and attitudes.

Technology

Technology means to apply science and engineering to practical needs. Agriculture had benefited greatly from Cyrus McCormick's reaper (1831), John Deere's steel plow (1837), and other inventions like threshing machines and corn planters. These improvements caused farmers to head west to states like Illinois, Indiana, and Michigan. From 1830 to 1860, the population of Indiana grew by 300%, Illinois by 1,000%, and Michigan by 2,300%. As farm production increased, it became possible to feed more people living in American cities and to export agricultural products to Europe.

Agriculture in New England could not compete with that in the West, but the Northeast's economy was saved by progress in the textile industry. In the mills of Lowell, Massachusetts, and other cities, cloth was produced from southern cotton and northern wool. Inventions created new opportunities for investment and employment: sewing machines, elevators, pneumatic tires, revolvers, and typesetting machines among them.

Growth of Cities

Cities grew rapidly in the North and were centers of both production and commerce. By 1860, over a million people lived in New York City; 565,000 in Philadelphia; 212,000 in Baltimore; and over 160,000 in both Cincinnati and St. Louis. City streets were clogged with wagons, carriages, and pedestrians. Poor immigrants fresh off the ship found rooms in city slums, where gangs and disease made their lives difficult.

Transportation and Communication

Transportation and communication had been improved greatly by new technology. To the dismay of those who owned turnpikes, stagecoaches, freight wagons, and steamboats, the railroads were coming on strong and taking their customers. In 1850, the northern states had about 6,500 miles of track, while the southern states had just over 2,000 miles of track. By 1861, the numbers had increased to 21,000 miles in the North and 9,500 miles in the South. Compared to the South, the North was far ahead; not only did it have more miles of track, but northern railroads were better equipped and maintained. The telegraph had been invented by Samuel F.B. Morse in 1841, and by 1860, there were 50,000 miles of line. The Trans-Atlantic cable was completed in 1858, but it broke a few months later.

Attitudes of the North and South

Attitudes were different in the North. People were more inclined toward reform movements; temperance, women's suffrage, and anti-slavery causes often drew the same individuals. Financial success was as important to Northerners as counting slaves and landholdings were to Southerners. Most Northerners saw change as something desirable, and even those who did not felt that it was inevitable. To them, southern preoccupation with slavery seemed hopelessly out of touch with reality.

Name: _____ Date: _____

Activity: Summarizing

Directions: Summarize the information in the reading selection for each category.

Technology	Transportation

Communications Networks	Attitudes

Events Leading Up to War

Stephen A. Douglas

It was not William Lloyd Garrison's *The Liberator* or southern nullifiers who created the Civil War. Most Americans were too busy working to worry much about these issues. By the 1840s, travel was mostly east to west, not north to south, so few in Georgia had ever met a New Yorker, and few Vermonters had ever met a Mississippian. Most Northerners weren't concerned about slavery and had no desire to either free slaves or have more slaves move to the north.

Slavery and Statehood

It was frontier expansion that caused Congress and the people to wrestle with the slavery question. It had been important in the question of whether to bring Texas into the Union and became more of an issue when the Mexican War began in 1846. At that time, Representative David Wilmot of Pennsylvania offered a proviso (condition) that slavery not be permitted in any territory taken from Mexico. The proviso passed in the House, but the Senate beat it back after Southerners warned it might lead to secession (leaving the United States). However, the issue did not die and came up frequently in Congress. The war ended as a great success in 1848; the United States gained 529,000 square miles of territory.

During the next year, thousands of Americans crossed the continent to find gold in California. By 1850, California had a population nearing 100,000, and it wanted statehood; but, if accepted, there would be more free states than slave states. The South would lose close Senate votes. Politicians now considered the slavery issue important, and some wanted to solve it.

Compromise of 1850

The aging Henry Clay, a member of the Whig Party, teamed up with ambitious young Stephen A. Douglas, a member of the Democratic Party, to piece together what became known as the Compromise of 1850. It included: California to be admitted as a free state, New Mexico and Utah Territories organized with no reference to slavery, a stronger fugitive slave law, an end to the slave trade in the District of Columbia, and Texas would receive $10 million in return for giving up some land to New Mexico. Debate was hot. Northerners like William Seward (New York) and Salmon Chase (Ohio) attacked it, but so did Jefferson Davis (Mississippi) and John C. Calhoun (South Carolina). Daniel Webster spoke in favor of the Compromise on March 7 and won over some Congressmen who were wavering on their vote. The Compromise was accepted; for a time, people felt better about the future of the United States.

Abolition Movement Gains Momentum

There were also people who wanted to end slavery on moral grounds and because they saw the suffering of the enslaved people. Publication of Harriet Beecher Stowe's novel *Uncle Tom's Cabin* in 1852 brought new converts to the abolition movement and made others wonder about how far they should go to cater to the South. Years later, Lincoln greeted Mrs. Stowe as "the little woman who made this big war."

Kansas-Nebraska Act

"Bleeding Kansas" also contributed to the war. In 1854, Senator Douglas proposed the Kansas-Nebraska bill, creating two new territories, each with the option to allow slavery if the people chose. Many Northerners protested this violation of the Missouri Compromise, which barred slavery from that region. The issue split Democrats, destroyed the Whigs, and created the Republican Party. The resulting tension led to an assault on Charles Sumner on the Senate floor and murders and raids in Kansas.

Name: _____ Date: _____

Activity: Event and Effect

Directions: What effect did each event have on the issue of slavery? Support your answers with details from the reading selection.

Slavery

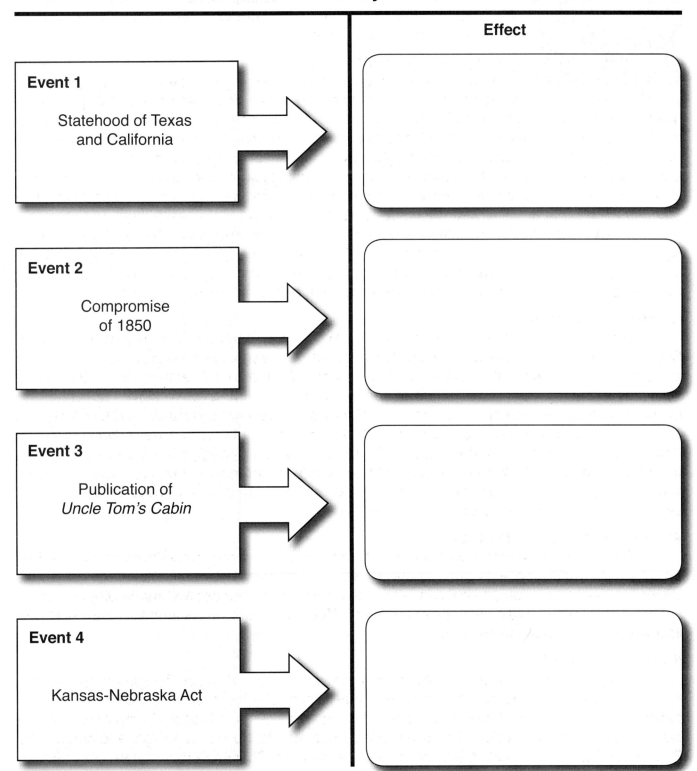

	Effect
Event 1 Statehood of Texas and California →	
Event 2 Compromise of 1850 →	
Event 3 Publication of *Uncle Tom's Cabin* →	
Event 4 Kansas-Nebraska Act →	

Dred Scott to John Brown (1857–1859)

In 1856, the nation elected its 15th president, James Buchanan. A man who had a hard time making decisions, his position was made more difficult by the four Southerners he picked for his Cabinet and by the Supreme Court. In 1857, three days after Buchanan took office, the Court handed down one of its most controversial decisions: *Dred Scott v. Sandford.*

Illustration depicting Dred Scott and his wife Harriet

Dred Scott v. Sanford

The *Dred Scott* case concerned a slave whose master, now dead, had taken him into territory declared free by the Missouri Compromise. Scott and his supporters felt this made him a free man, but the Missouri Supreme Court said it did not, and the case was appealed to the U.S. Supreme Court. Chief Justice Roger Taney handed down the majority decision. He said that Scott was not a citizen of Missouri or the United States, and the Missouri Compromise had been unconstitutional because territories existed "for the common use and equal benefit of all." The white South rejoiced that the Court agreed with them, but the ruling angered many Northerners. It hurt the image of the Court at a time when its influence was needed to protect civil rights.

The Lincoln-Douglas Debates

The Dred Scott issue spilled over into the election of 1858. Stephen Douglas's six-year term in the Senate was up that year, and since at that time state legislatures still elected senators, he needed a Democratic majority in the Illinois legislature so he could be reelected to the U.S. Senate. His Republican opponent was Abraham Lincoln, a Springfield attorney. Of the two, Douglas was by far the better known. Lincoln, a Whig turned Republican, appeared to be outclassed by the eloquent, well-dressed Douglas, but Douglas was not fooled. Lincoln had an appeal to the backwoods men of Illinois with his tall, rugged appearance and his clever sayings. The two held a series of debates, the most famous of which occurred at Freeport, Illinois. Lincoln asked Douglas if the people in a territory could exclude slavery. Douglas said they could keep it out by passing unfriendly laws. When the vote was held, Democrats kept control of the legislature and returned Douglas to the Senate. However, the debates made Lincoln famous and gave him a basis on which to run for president.

John Brown

John Brown returned to the nation's attention in 1859. A failure in most ways, he had often been forced to flee from bad debts. A strong abolitionist, Brown was angered because others talked but did nothing. He had gone to Kansas and raided a pro-slave community, brutally killing five men and boys. After a short stay in New England, he went to Missouri and stole 11 slaves and took them to Canada. He then planned an attack to free all slaves. After capturing the federal arsenal at Harpers Ferry, Virginia, he planned to arm the slaves in the area and begin a great revolt.

After the arsenal was captured, Brown's plan collapsed, and he was surrounded by militia and a company of marines led by army Colonel Robert E. Lee. Ten of Brown's men, including two of his sons, were killed when he refused to surrender. He was tried by the state, found guilty, and hanged. Some in the North said he was a hero, but others, including Lincoln, feared he had gone too far.

Name: _____ Date: _____

Activity: Summarizing

Directions: Use information from the reading selection to complete the graphic organizer.

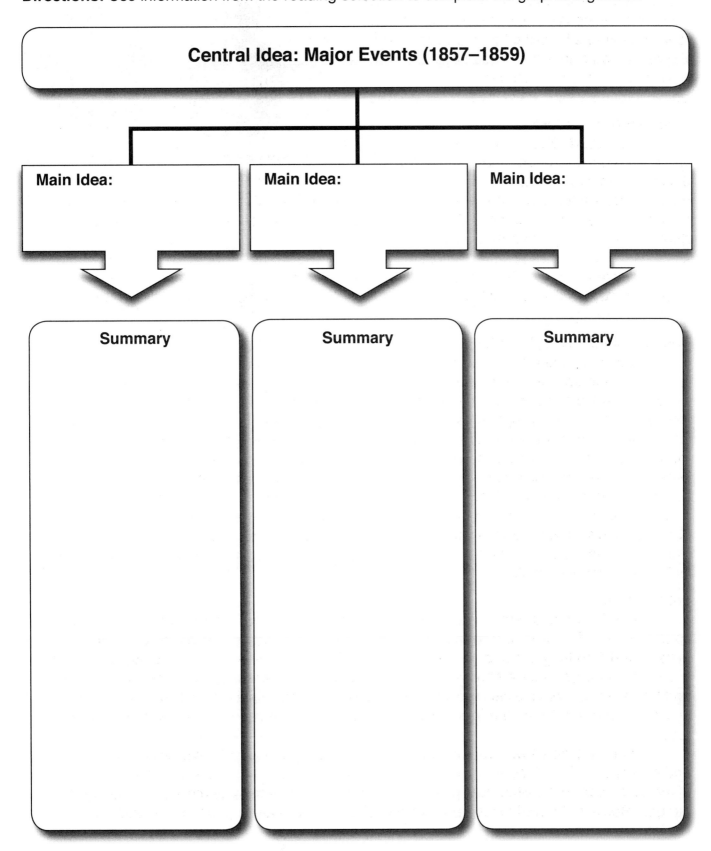

Central Idea: Major Events (1857–1859)

Main Idea:

Main Idea:

Main Idea:

Summary

Summary

Summary

The 1860 Election and the Secession Crisis

By 1860, the aftermath of John Brown's raid was felt across the nation. President Buchanan's image was hurt by scandals in his administration, and the Supreme Court was discredited because of the *Dred Scott* decision. Congress was hardly

Presidential and Vice-Presidential Candidates in 1860: Republicans—Abraham Lincoln and Hannibal Hamlin, Northern Democrats—Stephen Douglas and Herschel Johnson, Southern Democrats—John Breckenridge and Joseph Lane, Constitutional Union Party—John Bell and Edward Everett

able to do business; anything one section proposed was opposed by members from the other section. Chaos was taking over.

All of this made the election of 1860 especially important. The Democrats met in Charleston, South Carolina, in April, and even though Stephen Douglas was popular with Northern delegates, he lacked Southern support. The convention adjourned without choosing a candidate and decided to meet in June at Baltimore. Members of the Whig and Know-Nothing Parties joined forces that year and relabeled themselves as the Constitutional Union Party. They chose John Bell of Tennessee and Edward Everett of Massachusetts as their candidates.

The Republican convention met in Chicago. Two men had the largest delegate support: Abraham Lincoln and William Seward. The party platform (policies) was written first, and it included the right of states to control slavery, a railroad to the Pacific, a homestead act, and a protective tariff. The contest for president was hard fought, but Lincoln won the nomination on the third ballot. The vice presidential choice was Hannibal Hamlin of Maine.

When Democrats met again at Baltimore, they were no closer to agreement than they had been in Charleston. Southern delegates walked out; the Northern delegates then chose Douglas as their presidential candidate. Southerners met again and chose John C. Breckinridge of Kentucky as their candidate.

Secession Crisis

There were no TV commercials or presidential debates in 1860 and very few speeches by the candidates. Southerners warned they would leave the Union if Lincoln was elected. That threat had been used before, and few Republicans believed Southerners were serious. Douglas, however, did believe them and campaigned in the South warning against the folly of secession.

Lincoln won a clear majority in the electoral vote with 180, Breckinridge 72, Bell 39, and Douglas 12. Lincoln won in Northern states, Douglas and Bell in Border States, and Breckinridge in the South.

Receiving promises of support from Mississippi and Alabama, South Carolina seceded from the Union on December 20, 1860. In South Carolina, people cheered and bands played as the U.S. flag was taken down. Other states of the Deep South felt the same joy as they departed in January 1861. The Union was falling apart, and Buchanan was still president until March.

Buchanan did not know what to do. He opposed secession but felt he had no right to force states to remain in the Union. Many Cabinet members, military people, and government employees supported the South, so no one could be trusted. By March 1861, seven states had left the Union and seized all federal property within their borders. Now only two spots remained in Federal hands: Fort Sumter in Charleston's harbor and Fort Pickens at Pensacola, Florida.

Name: _____ Date: _____

Activity: Recalling Information

Directions: Use information from the reading selection to complete the graphic organizer.

1. Who were the four presidential candidates and which party did each represent?

2. What four issues were included in the Republican Party Platform?

Election of 1860 and the Secession Crisis

3. Why did the Democratic Party have two presidential candidates?

4. What was President Buchanan's reaction to the secession crisis?

Attack on Fort Sumter

The bombardment of Fort Sumter

As Abraham Lincoln made the journey from Illinois to Washington, D.C., he gave no indication as to how he planned to handle the situation at Fort Sumter in South Carolina. The federal fort had not yet been seized by the South, even though Major Robert Anderson and his men were within range of South Carolina cannons in Charleston Harbor and were running out of food and supplies. In his inaugural address on March 4, 1861, Lincoln said it was up to the South to decide if there would be war; at the end, he said: "I am loath to close. We are not enemies but friends. We must not be enemies." This appeal was directed mostly to the loyal citizens of the border slave states who were watching and deciding which way they should go if fighting began at Fort Sumter.

Lincoln moved very slowly at first, waiting for Unionist sentiment to develop in states like Virginia, Maryland, Kentucky, and Missouri. His lack of action caused even Cabinet members to wonder if he was up to the job. The South was also waiting, hopeful that he would surrender Fort Sumter without a fight and let the South leave the Union without a war.

Patience was wearing thin on both sides, and the new Confederate president, Jefferson Davis, feared that South Carolina would soon act on its own unless he pressured Anderson to leave Fort Sumter. On April 10, General P.G.T. Beauregard was sent orders to demand the fort's surrender. On April 12, Beauregard sent officers to the fort, and Anderson told them he would run out of supplies in a few days unless he was resupplied. Beauregard seized the opportunity and told Anderson firing would begin on the fort in one hour. At 4:30 A.M., shelling began and continued for 30 long hours. Anderson surrendered the fort on April 14, and he and his men were allowed to leave by ship.

On April 15, President Lincoln called on governors to supply 75,000 militia volunteers who would serve 90-day enlistments. Governors of the Border States now faced the moment of truth. Would they commit their men to a war against their friends in the South and support a Federal government that, in the view of many, threatened states' rights and the institution of slavery?

Southern Unionists were in an uphill battle to influence their states' decisions. They felt that the Federal government must guarantee states' rights. Following Lincoln's call for state militia volunteers to help put down the rebellion, four more Southern states left the Union: Virginia (April 17), Arkansas (May 6), North Carolina (May 20), and Tennessee (June 8). Governor John Ellis of North Carolina wrote Lincoln: "I can be no party to this wicked violation of the laws of the country and to this war upon the liberties of a free people." The Confederacy had grown from seven to eleven states.

Did You Know?

On January 5, 1861, a civilian ship, *Star of the West,* was sent to resupply Fort Sumter. The mission was abandoned on January 9 when South Carolina militia cannons fired upon the supply ship, forcing it to turn around.

Many in the other four slave states (Delaware, Maryland, Kentucky, and Missouri) also wanted to secede, but Lincoln was determined to use any means to keep them from leaving the Union. Delaware legislators voted against succession on January 3, 1861. Governor Beriah Magoffin of Kentucky declared his state neutral and refused to send state militia to aid either side. Maryland's governor was loyal, but many in the legislature were not, and 19 were arrested. Governor Claiborne Jackson of Missouri wanted secession, but Unionists were strong enough in the state to prevent him from succeeding.

Name: _____ Date: _____

Activity: Sequence of Events

Directions: Use information from the reading selection to record the sequence of events beginning with Lincoln's inaugural address to the secession of Tennessee.

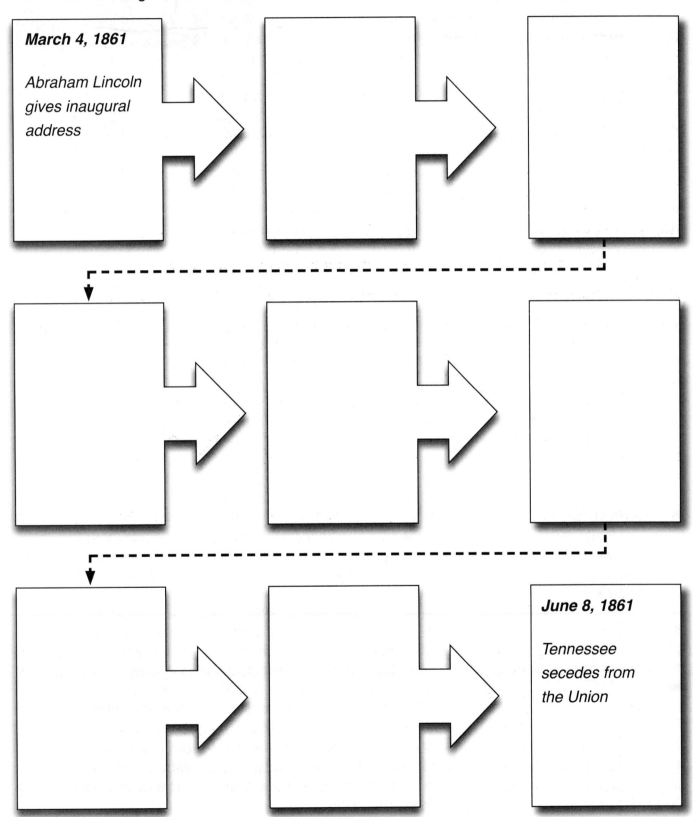

March 4, 1861

Abraham Lincoln gives inaugural address

June 8, 1861

Tennessee secedes from the Union

Abraham Lincoln vs. Jefferson Davis

Jefferson Davis

Jefferson Davis was disappointed when he was chosen president of the Confederate States of America (CSA). Unlike Lincoln, who had worked hard to become president of the United States, Davis did not want the job; he would have much preferred being a general. His wife, Varina, wrote that his main talent was military: "He did not know the arts of the politician and would not practice them if understood."

Abraham Lincoln (left), President of the United States; Jefferson Davis (right), President of the Confederate States of America

In experience, Davis had an impressive record. Educated at Transylvania University and West Point, he had been an army officer in the Northwest and was wounded in battle during the Mexican War. His legislative career included terms in both the House and Senate. In 1853, he became Secretary of War. He returned to the Senate in 1857, where he remained until 1861. He opposed secession, but after the decision was made, he supported it.

Abraham Lincoln

Lincoln's record was shorter. Born in Kentucky, his family had migrated to Illinois. He never attended college, but he read enough to qualify as a lawyer. His military service was a brief stint as a militia captain during the Black Hawk War in 1832. He wrote that he never even saw an Indian and never bent a sword in battle, but he had many bloody encounters with mosquitoes and bent his musket once by accident. He had served four terms in the Illinois state legislature and one term in the U.S. House of Representatives.

Perhaps the greatest compliment paid to Lincoln during his lifetime was by the Southern newspaper, the Charleston *Mercury,* which said that he ran the presidency with "a bold, steady hand, a vigilant, active eye, a sleepless energy, a fanatic spirit ... and a singleness of purpose that might almost be called patriotic."

Comparing Lincoln and Davis

In some ways the two men faced similar situations. Both came under fire from the press and were accused of acting like dictators. Each had a Congress that seemed more concerned about getting friends into high places and offering unhelpful suggestions than winning the war. Each wasted valuable time at long Cabinet meetings instead of letting the heads of departments do their jobs. Each showed personal courage in dangerous situations. Lincoln walked through the streets of Washington accompanied by only one bodyguard, even though there were many rumors of plots against his life. Davis tried to stop bread rioters in Richmond by himself. Both men carried the burden of long casualty lists and many citizens accusing them of not doing everything possible to end the conflict.

The main difference between the two was that Lincoln was far superior as a politician. Often exhausted and tense, he listened carefully to those who lined up outside his office "for a brief word." He visited military hospitals, shaking hands with the troops, knowing that their relatives voted. Lincoln often delayed making decisions until public opinion was strongly behind the policy he intended to pursue in the first place. Davis did not play the political game, stubbornly pushing unpopular policies.

Name: _____ Date: _____

Activity: Compare and Contrast

Directions: Use information from the reading selection to complete the graphic organizer.

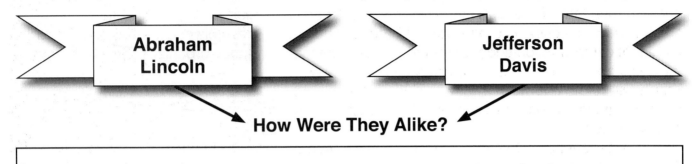

| Abraham Lincoln | | Jefferson Davis |

How Were They Alike?

How Were They Different?

Abraham Lincoln   Jefferson Davis

	Education	
	Military Experience	
	Political Life	
	Attitude Toward Presidency	

Organizing the Two Armies

In the weeks following secession, both the Union and Confederacy issued a call to arms and began a mad rush to organize their growing numbers of untried volunteers into effective armies. The net result was two American armies, both composed mainly of volunteer units. The two armies were similar in structure. The Union Army had an established way of organizing its forces. Since many Confederate officers came out of that army, they organized the same way.

Territorial Departments

Both armies were organized into Territorial Departments (the area where they would be used) and then into smaller units. Confederate armies were named after the state or the region in which they operated. One Confederate Army was the Army of Tennessee, for example. The Union armies were named after the major river flowing near where they operated. It had an Army of <u>the</u> Tennessee. Both sides then had smaller units that operated inside this larger "army."

> **Did You Know?**
>
> When orders came for a unit to move, the whole community turned out; bands played, flags flew, and there were tearful farewells, as the town saluted its brave young heroes marching off to war.

Companies

The smallest unit was the company. Companies were hometown volunteer units, with most members coming from the same town or county. This would make the horror of war very real when the company suffered heavy losses in battle. In the Union Army, companies had from 83 to 101 officers and men. Confederate companies were not so tightly controlled. Company officers included a captain, two lieutenants, five sergeants, eight corporals, and a teamster (wagon driver). Early in the war, the men elected company officers, but by 1862, both armies held examinations to choose officers. This weeded out incompetents and appointed better-qualified men to lead the units.

Regiments

Regiments were composed of companies. Infantry regiments contained 10 companies, but cavalry regiments were composed of 12. In both armies, regiments were commanded by a colonel; other officers were a lieutenant colonel, major, adjutant (assistant to the commander), quartermaster, three surgeons, and a chaplain. As the war continued, new soldiers were not put into old regiments, but new regiments were formed. Regiments were numbered by the order in which they formed and their state; for example, the 3rd Vermont Cavalry, or 5th Virginia Infantry.

Brigades, Divisions, and Corps

Brigades were composed of two or more regiments, with both armies assigning four or five regiments to a brigade. In the Union Army, brigades were numbered (3rd Brigade), while Confederates named their brigades after their commanding officer (Hood's Brigade). In both armies, brigades were commanded by a brigadier general.

Divisions were made up of two or more brigades. Divisions were commanded by staff officers, major generals, or lieutenant generals.

Corps (pronounced "cores") were made up of at least two divisions, with three being the most common. They were given Roman numerals to identify them, such as III Corps. In the Union Army, major generals commanded them; in the Confederate Army, lieutenant generals were the commanders.

Name: _____ Date: _____

Activity: Making a Comparison

Directions: Use the T-Chart to compare the organization of the Union and Confederate armies

Union Army	Confederate Army

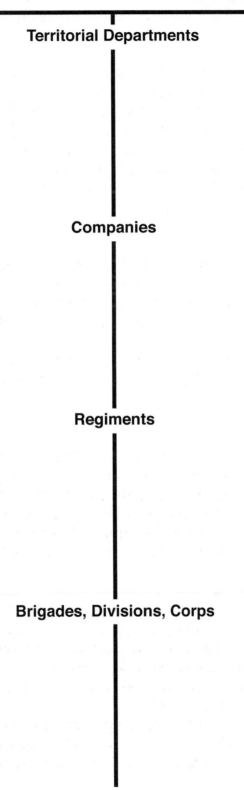

Territorial Departments

Companies

Regiments

Brigades, Divisions, Corps

The Instruments of War

By the time of the American Civil War, European armies had defined the roles of the three major branches of warfare. It remained only for the leaders of the two American armies to adapt these roles to their struggle. With minor differences, the Union and Confederate armies used them in the same ways.

Union artilery park in Yorktown, Virginia

Infantry

The infantry was the backbone of both armies. War, in the 19th century, was a "stand up and shoot it out" affair. Both armies maneuvered their troops into battle lines at ranges of 300 yards or less and swept the enemy line with thousands of large-caliber musket balls. Firing was normally "by the book," with officers ordering their men to "load-aim-fire" in separate commands. In this way, they controlled the timing as well as the volume of fire. This is referred to as "firing by volleys." Many soldiers were poor shots, and controlled firing by thousands of muskets at the same time had a way of making up for bad marksmanship.

Hours were spent drilling infantrymen according to the *Manual of Arms,* teaching the soldier to handle his musket the same way every time he loaded and fired. After many drills, every man did the same thing at the same time. Much time was spent teaching soldiers to march and maneuver in unison. Moving large numbers of men into position in the heat of battle was as important as actually firing at the enemy. Once in position, the usual practice for the attacking army was to fire several volleys, then charge, using bayonets attached to the muzzles of the muskets. When a charge began, it was impossible for the defenders to get off more than one or two volleys, so everything depended on the courage of both armies.

The last moments of the charge were always the most critical, since it always ended in hand-to-hand combat. After the battle, bodies of dead and injured infantrymen littered the battlefield.

Artillery

Artillery was vital to a battle. Civil War cannons had a fairly short range (1,500–2,500 yards for most), but they could reach the enemy at longer distances than muskets. If a defending general had enough cannons, he might break up a charge before it got close enough to succeed. Artillery fired a variety of shells: solid cannonballs, explosive shells (shrapnel), or canisters (small iron balls). In a siege, artillery had a deadly effect—lobbing exploding shells into the enemy line, day and night if necessary.

Cavalry

The cavalry consisted of mounted soldiers who could do many things. They were lightly equipped and lightly armed, so they could move quickly. Weapons included a revolver and saber for mounted fighting and a short rifle (carbine) for fighting on foot. General Lee called the cavalry "the eyes of my army" and used it to scout Union positions. Cavalry also rode rapidly to support infantry, dismounting and filling gaps in the line when they arrived. Because cannons were so hard to turn, cavalry could charge at artillery positions from the side, kill the gun crews, and capture the guns.

Activity: Research

To learn more about the organization of the Civil War armies, go online to <https://www.youtube.com/watch?v=DgqHXVTYfl0> to view the video, *The Civil War in Four Minutes: Army Organization.*

Name: _____ Date: _____

Activity: Recalling Information

Directions: Answer the questions using information from the reading selection.

1. What branch was called the "backbone of the army"?

2. What was the critical point in an infantry charge? Why?

3. What were two uses for artillery?

4. What was the range of most Civil War cannons?

5. Why did Lee call the cavalry the "eyes of my army"?

6. Why might a cavalryman be used on foot in battles?

Bull Run: The First Major Test of the War

After Fort Sumter fell, most Americans, North and South, believed the war would be short, with one major battle deciding the outcome. When the Confederate States of America (CSA) chose Richmond, Virginia, as its capital, it seemed certain that the clash would occur somewhere in the 100 miles that separated the Confederate capital from Washington, D.C. The Confederates established a defensive line along Bull Run Creek to shield an important railroad junction at Manassas, Virginia.

Ruins of Stone Bridge, Bull Run, Virginia

The new Union Army of 39,000 men created by President Lincoln's call for 90-day volunteers was commanded by General Irvin McDowell. General Robert Patterson also had 11,000 men to threaten Harpers Ferry, Virginia. In June, Confederate General P.G.T. Beauregard, victor at Fort Sumter, took command of the Bull Run line, while General Joseph Johnston guarded Harpers Ferry.

Time was running out for Lincoln's 90-day army, and Washington politicians were spoiling for a fight. McDowell pleaded for more time but was ordered to move by late July. "On to Richmond!" was the slogan of the day. Patterson's troops captured Harpers Ferry in early July, and Beauregard braced for an attack. McDowell marched into Virginia on July 16, 1861. The weather was brutally hot, and his new soldiers were soft. McDowell rested his men at Fairfax Courthouse on the 17th. The 18th and 19th were spent at Centerville while he perfected his battle plan and chose the 21st as the day of attack.

While McDowell delayed, Beauregard gathered his forces and waited. On the 18th, Johnston was ordered to move his troops to Manassas Junction. When Johnston arrived with half of his troops, he took command of the Confederate forces there. All of Johnston's field commanders were either West Point graduates or Mexican War veterans. McDowell's officers were not as well trained and experienced.

Instead of a mass attack, McDowell attempted a series of small frontal attacks. The Southerners divided their duties, with Beauregard directing the defense and Johnston sending fresh troops where they were needed. The attack began early on the morning of the 21st, but McDowell's efforts were hampered by picnickers out to watch the glorious battle. His wagons had a hard time moving through the carriages of the sightseers.

At first it seemed McDowell's attack would succeed. Colonel David Hunter's 6,000 men crossed Bull Run Creek at Sudley Springs Ford and drove three Confederate brigades back. The three retreating Confederate brigades climbed Henry House Hill, where they found Confederate General Thomas Jackson waiting patiently with a full brigade in battle formation. General Barnard Bee stopped the retreating troops, shouting: "There stands Jackson, like a stone wall." The three brigades joined Jackson's line. McDowell ordered two artillery batteries to soften up the Southern line at Henry House Hill, but they were wiped out. At 3:30 P.M., two fresh Confederate brigades attacked McDowell's right flank (side). Beauregard then ordered a general attack, and by 4 P.M., McDowell's Union Army was in retreat. Chaos took over as carriages and cannons, soldiers and picnickers scrambled back to Washington; however, Johnston did not pursue because his men were too tired and disorganized to follow.

Name: _____ Date: _____

Activity: Supporting Details

Directions: Answer the questions. Support your answer using details from the reading selection.

1. What advantage did Confederate General Johnston's officers have over Union General McDowell's officers?

2. Why do you think spectators came to view the battle?

3. What important role did General Thomas Jackson and his men play in the battle?

Formation of the Confederacy

Confederate Government

How do you start a government from scratch, knowing that war may be fast approaching? As leaders from Southern states gathered in Montgomery, Alabama, in February 1861, there was little time for original thinking, and they hurriedly wrote a constitution similar to that of the United States. Jefferson Davis was chosen as provisional president, and the vice presidency went to Alexander Stephens of Georgia. Stephens, instead of helping Davis, often worked against him and criticized Davis's policies.

In May 1861, the capital was moved to Richmond, Virginia, a larger city with a more comfortable climate. Only about 100 miles from Washington, D.C., Richmond was also important because of its Tredegar Iron Works. The Union's struggle to capture Richmond and the South's determination to hold it made that decision important in the story of eastern campaigns (battles).

Confederate Uniforms

The militia units making up the Confederate Army were dressed in almost every style of uniform. The official color was cadet gray, but not enough dye was available to have all units dressed the same. Many soldiers dressed in butternut-colored uniforms (made by boiling nut shells and iron oxide filings). Most men dressed in whatever they came with or could afford. Even generals rarely dressed in fancy uniforms. The soap shortage made cleanliness an extravagance, and many were without winter coats, blankets, shoes, or boots. Like the Union Army, cavalry wore yellow stripes on their pants, artillery wore red, and infantry wore blue.

Confederate Flags

The first official flag was the "Stars and Bars," (blue field in the left corner, a white stripe between two red stripes). At Bull Run, General Beauregard saw flags of new troops arriving, but could not tell whether they carried Union or Confederate flags. That caused a battle flag to be adopted in September 1861. It had a red field with a large blue X, and it is the flag most commonly associated with the Confederacy. Meanwhile, the "Stars and Bars" was still being used, but its similarity to the "Stars and Stripes" caused confusion, so in 1863, the "Stainless Banner," with a battle flag in the upper left corner and a white field was adopted. However, when there was no wind, it looked like a flag of truce, so the "Last National" flag was adopted in March 1865; it had a broad red bar across the end of the Stainless Banner.

Confederate Economy

Two other decisions affected the South's economy. One was to borrow money rather than tax the citizens. People were not used to paying taxes directly to Washington, and their loyalty at this point was seen as more important than their money. Instead of taxing, the Confederacy would borrow by selling bonds. Then they started printing Confederate currency without any official gold or silver reserves to back the money. When the South won battles at the war's beginning, people accepted the money, but after disasters in 1863, it became almost worthless.

Another important decision was to stop selling cotton to Europe. The idea was to cause mass unemployment at European textile mills and force England and France to recognize Confederate independence. It did cause some unemployment in English textile mills, but its greatest effect was to hurt the South's ability to buy supplies and arms.

Name: _____ Date: _____

Activity: Key Details

Directions: Use information from the reading selection to complete the graphic organizer.

Confederate

Key Details

Government

Uniforms

Flag

Economy

President Lincoln Orders a Coastal Blockade

President Lincoln's choice for Secretary of the Navy was politician and newspaper editor Gideon Welles. Hard-working, focused on the task he faced, and totally loyal to Lincoln, he made an excellent Cabinet member. His chief assistant was Gustavus Fox, a former naval officer. Together, they took on many difficult assignments during the war. The navy gave support to military operations and was vital to the success of Grant, Butler, and others. The main task of the ocean navy was to keep cotton from leaving the South and arms and supplies from coming into Southern ports.

Ships of this type were used by blockade runners to smuggle goods in and out of the South.

Union Blockades the Coastline

Five days after Fort Sumter fell, Lincoln ordered a blockade from South Carolina to Texas. After Virginia and North Carolina seceded, their coastlines were included. The purpose was to keep the Confederacy from shipping its products to foreign ports and, more importantly, to keep arms and needed supplies from reaching the South. The job was easier said than done. The area covered totaled 3,550 miles. The U.S. Navy had 90 ships (only 42 of which were in commission). Three ships were in the East Indies, and 23 were in the Pacific. Obviously, the blockade would be useless until the navy was greatly enlarged, and that was exactly what Welles set out to do. He recruited 20,000 sailors from merchant ships and purchased 100 boats of all varieties; the only requirement was they must be able to support guns.

Another task was to capture harbors on the Confederate coastline that the blockaders could use for coal and supplies. Port Royal, between Charleston and Savannah, was captured and became a supply base for the blockaders.

At first, it was easy for ships to run the blockade, but in time it began to tighten and forced the South to find new ways to break it.

The Confederate Response

The Confederate counterpart to Welles was Stephen Mallory, former senator from Florida and perhaps the most original thinker in the Cabinet. His task was to find ways to break the blockade with very little expense. He took the sunken steamer *Merrimac* and turned it into the ironclad CSS *Virginia*. The Confederacy also tried building submarines. The first attempts were unsuccessful, and many crewmen's lives were lost. But eventually the submarine CSS *Hunley* sank the USS *Housatonic* by use of a mine attached to a long pole. The explosion, however, also destroyed the *Hunley*.

Commerce raiders were sent out to attack Northern shipping to force the navy to pull ships out of the blockade line to chase them. Some raiders were very successful. The CSS *Alabama,* commanded by Raphael Semmes, captured or destroyed 64 vessels, including a Union gunboat. The CSS *Shenandoah* was the only Confederate ship to go around the world, and it captured 30 ships. In total, the raiders captured 200 ships, with damages of $15 to 20 million.

Fast, long, and sleek blockade runners were privately owned and carried needed supplies to the Confederacy. As the blockade tightened, many were captured. Welles had won the contest, but Mallory had proven himself a worthy competitor.

Name: _____ Date: _____

Activity: Recalling Information

Directions: Use information from the reading selection to complete the graphic organizer

Union Blockades Coastline	**The Confederate Response**
Who?	**Who?**
What?	**What?**
When?	**Why?**
Where?	**How?**
Why?	

Fort Henry and Fort Donelson

Ulysses S. Grant, who had left the army in 1854, returned in 1861 with the help of political pull. No one could have guessed what a major part he was destined to play in the Civil War. His fame spread rapidly after his first two battles at Fort Henry and Fort Donelson. Three important water routes flowed north to south, cutting into the western part of the Confederacy: the Mississippi, Tennessee, and Cumberland Rivers. To discourage invasion, the Confederacy fortified "Island Number 10" on the Mississippi, Fort Henry on the Tennessee, and Fort Donelson on the Cumberland. These water routes were too tempting for the Union to ignore. In February 1862, Brigadier General Grant began planning to open the Tennessee and Cumberland Rivers to Union shipping.

Ulysses S. Grant

Fort Henry

Naval Flag Officer Andrew Foote commanded the gunboats that supported Grant's attacks. Two full divisions of troops aboard steamboats were covered by seven gunboats. The Union troops were landed four miles from Fort Henry, and on February 6, 1862, the gunboats attacked the fort. Heavy rains had raised the river's level, and Fort Henry was partly flooded. The fort's commander, General Lloyd Tilghman, had sent most of his troops to Fort Donelson, 12 miles away, keeping only a few artillerymen to defend the fort. Taking advantage of the high water, Foote's gunboats came so close to Fort Henry that many of the fort's guns could not be turned on the gunboats. At point-blank range, he hammered the fort for two hours. Outgunned and undermanned, Tilghman surrendered. The Tennessee River was open to Union attack all the way into Alabama.

Fort Donelson

Fort Donelson was not as easy. It lay on high ground and was well fortified. It had 21,000 defenders to take on Grant's 15,000 men, but Foote's gunboats evened up the odds. Foote attacked on February 14, but his guns did little damage to the fort. The fort's guns found their mark, sinking two gunboats and damaging the rest. Grant called off the attack and moved his troops in for a siege. The weather was very cold, and Grant's men burrowed into the fall leaves to keep warm. Grant needed help to succeed, and fortunately for him, it came from the Confederate commanders at the fort.

Confederate General Gideon Pillow attempted to break through Grant's lines and open a path to Nashville, Tennessee. Colonel Nathan Bedford Forrest's cavalry led the attack over the snow; by noon, he had cleared the way, but Pillow lost his nerve and returned to the fort. Inside the fort, tempers flared. Forrest was naturally furious with Pillow for retreating. General John Floyd, acting Post Commander, gave in to Pillow in the dispute, and Floyd and Pillow decided to surrender the fort. Since neither of them wanted that responsibility, they passed it on to General Simon Buckner, the third man in charge. Forrest vowed he would never quit and took his 700 cavalrymen out before Buckner could meet with Grant.

When Buckner asked for the terms, Grant answered: "unconditional surrender." Newspapers became excited by that statement and printed glowing accounts of this new general who had brought home two major victories.

Name: _____ Date: _____

Activity: Analyzing a Primary Source

Directions: Read the following excerpts taken from the *Personal Memoirs of U.S. Grant*. Then answer the questions below.

Excerpt One

"On the 7th, the day after the fall of Fort Henry, I took my staff and the cavalry—a part of one regiment—and made a reconnaissance [sic] to within about a mile of the outer line of works at Donelson. I had known General Pillow in Mexico, and judged that with any force, no matter how small, I could march up to within gunshot of any intrenchments [sic] he was given to hold. I said this to the officers of my staff at the time. I knew that Floyd was in command, but he was no soldier, and I judged that he would yield to Pillow's pretensions."

Excerpt Two

"I had been at West Point three years with Buckner and afterwards served with him in the army, so that we were quite well acquainted. In the course of our conversation, which was very friendly, he said to me that if he had been in command I would not have got up to Donelson as easily as I did. I told him that if he had been in command I should not have tried in the way I did: I had invested their lines with a smaller force than they had to defend them, and at the same time had sent a brigade full 5,000 strong, around by water; I had relied very much upon their commander to allow me to come safely up to the outside of their works."

1. According to the excerpts, what was Grant's opinion of the Confederate Generals Floyd, Pillow, and Buckner?

   _____

   _____

   _____

   _____

2. How are Grant's views of the Confederate generals supported by the information in the reading selection?

   _____

   _____

   _____

   _____

Merrimac vs. *Monitor*: Battle of the Ironclads

The Confederacy began the war without a navy, but its secretary of war, Stephen Mallory, began early to correct that problem by building ironclads.

Merrimac Renamed CSS *Virginia*

When the Union abandoned its shipyard at Norfolk, Virginia, they burned and left behind a steamship called the *Merrimac*. Confederate engineers raised the hull, which had not burned below the waterline. Renamed the CSS *Virginia*, the entire ship was covered with heavy iron plates, and it was armed with 10 heavy cannons capable of firing 100-pound shells. With its armor, guns, and powerful steam engines, it was more powerful than any Union ship. News of its construction caused panic in Washington. Assistant Secretary of the Navy Gustavus Fox asked: "Who is to stop her from steaming up the Potomac and throwing her hundred-pound shells into the White House, or battering down the hall of Congress?"

USS *Monitor*

"Who" turned out to be Swedish-born inventor John Ericsson. Secretary of the Navy Gideon Welles begged him to do something to stop the CSS *Virginia*. Ericsson designed a strange looking ship resembling a rectangle-shaped box on a raft. The USS *Monitor* had a low, flat deck with a small rotating turret in the center that contained two guns. She was launched January 30, 1862, just 101 days after plans left the drawing board. The design was radical, and she was not very seaworthy. The *Monitor* was modified and finally sailed out of New York Harbor headed for the Virginia coastline.

On Saturday, March 8, 1862, laundry was being washed and hung to dry on the rigging of ships blockading the Virginia coastline. The *Virginia* chose this as the day to come out and fight. She plowed through the water toward the USS *Cumberland*. The *Cumberland's* captain described the *Virginia* as resembling a crocodile with an iron hide and guns and a long ram projecting forward. The *Cumberland* opened fire, but its cannon balls bounced off the *Virginia's* iron hull. The *Virginia* rammed the *Cumberland*, splintering her wooden hull, then opened fire at point-blank range. The *Cumberland's* guns were still firing as she sank beneath the waves. The *Virginia* then destroyed the USS *Congress* and drove the USS *Minnesota* aground before withdrawing for the night. The crew decided the *Virginia* could finish off the *Minnesota* in the morning.

At 1 A.M. the next morning, the worried sailors on the deck of the *Minnesota* saw the *Monitor* pull alongside. Six hours later, the *Virginia* returned to destroy the *Minnesota,* but found a new opponent in her way. For four and one half hours, the ironclads battled in the shallow waters off Hampton Roads, Virginia. The ships were so close they collided five times, while the men loaded and fired as fast as they could. Finally, the *Virginia* withdrew after ruling the sea only one day. In their struggle, these two iron ships made every wooden naval ship in the world obsolete.

Neither ship fought again. The *Virginia* was blown up by the Confederates two months later to keep her from being captured. The *Monitor* sank in a storm off Cape Hatteras, North Carolina, in December 1862. After revolutionizing naval warfare, the two ships disappeared, but their memories linger on.

Activity: Research

To learn more about the battle of the ironclads, read *Duel of the Ironclads: the Monitor Vs. the Virginia* by Patrick O'Brien.

Name: _____ Date: _____

Activity: Making Inferences

An **inference** is a conclusion a reader makes based on reliable evidence and reasoning rather than from explicit statements in the reading selection.

Directions: Think about what you learned from the reading selection and what you already know. Then answer the questions below. Support your answers with details and examples.

1. Do you think the commander of the CSS *Virginia* made a mistake by waiting until the next morning to destroy the USS *Minnesota*?

2. What impact, if any, do you think the CSS *Virginia* had on the Civil War during its one day of sea battles?

McClellan's Peninsular Campaign of 1862

Bull Run showed the North that a long war lay ahead of them. The aged General Winfield Scott was replaced by General George McClellan as commander in chief of the North's army. He improved the men's spirits and organized the broken volunteer force into an effective army.

Battery No. 1, near Yorktown, Virginia, May 1862

Washington and Richmond were separated by only 100 miles, and each side shaped its plans around capturing the other's capital. McClellan wanted to try reaching Richmond by attacking from the east rather than the north. He did not want to move until his army was much larger than that of the Confederates; the problem was that in his mind, the South's army was always much larger than it actually was. President Lincoln finally ordered him to attack, and on March 17, 1862, McClellan moved 12 divisions by ship to Fort Monroe on the tip of the peninsula formed by the James and York Rivers.

Reaction of Confederate Generals

To prevent more Union troops from joining McClellan, Confederate General Robert E. Lee suggested that General "Stonewall" Jackson threaten the Union armies in the Shenandoah Valley. Moving so quickly they became known as "Jackson's foot cavalry," Jackson's troops caught the Union Army by surprise one time after another. Jackson then rejoined the main Confederate force facing McClellan.

Union troops began moving toward Richmond on April 4, but found their way blocked the next day by Confederate-made earthworks thrown up by General John Magruder's small army of 10,000 men. Even though McClellan had a larger army, he waited for more men to arrive before ordering a siege. That gave the Confederates time to move most of their soldiers in the region to oppose him. General Joe Johnston was given command of the Confederate's Yorktown line. McClellan prepared to attack that line, but by the time he was ready, Johnston's army had pulled back to stronger positions near Richmond. McClellan moved his base up to West Point, at the head of the York River. McClellan divided his army, with some north and others south of the Chickahominy River.

Johnston saw this as an opportunity and attacked Union troops south of the river at Fair Oaks. Johnston was seriously wounded, so command of the army was given to Robert E. Lee. Lee sent General Jeb Stuart with 1,200 cavalrymen to discover enemy positions and strength. Stuart rode behind McClellan's army, gathered information, tore up a railroad, took prisoners, and with his mission completed, led his men back around the enemy. McClellan was so shocked by this that he moved all but the V Corps south of the river and built defenses at White Oak Swamp.

Lee took advantage of McClellan's caution. He called his generals together: Jackson, Longstreet, and A.P. Hill. He decided to send most of the army to crush the V Corps north of the river. Once it was destroyed, McClellan would have to retreat, ending the threat to Richmond. The risk in the plan was that by moving his troops north of the river, he could only leave 20,000 men south of it; they would be outnumbered by 70,000 Union troops. Considering McClellan's reluctance to act, Lee took the risk.

Name: _____ Date: _____

Activity: Summarizing

Directions: Use information from the reading selection to complete the graphic organizer.

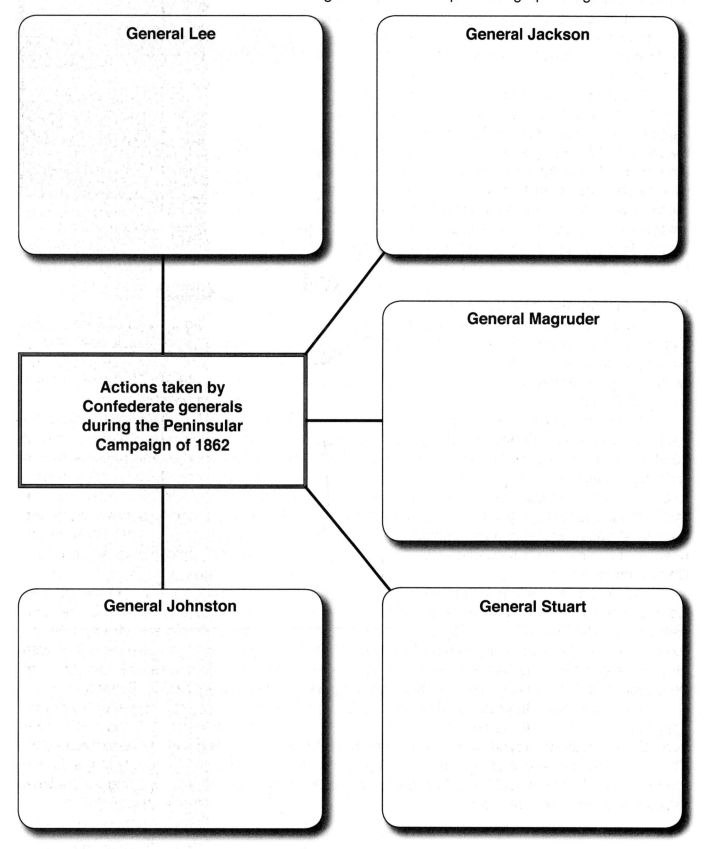

General Lee

General Jackson

General Magruder

Actions taken by Confederate generals during the Peninsular Campaign of 1862

General Johnston

General Stuart

The Confederate High Command

In the early days of the war, both North and South struggled to find generals who could lead armies into battle and win. By 1862, the Confederacy had found a group of officers able to produce victories, even without having all the supplies their opponents had.

Robert Edward Lee (1807–1870) of Virginia, son of a Revolutionary War hero, graduated second in his West Point class and served in the Mexican War. In 1860, he was a colonel, U.S. 1st Cavalry, and was offered command of the Union Army, but refused it when Virginia seceded. He resigned his commission to serve the South. By war's end, he was commander in chief of the Confederate Army. Lee proved to be a capable field commander who had an amazing ability to think on the move and outguess his opponent. One has to wonder how different the war would have been if he had taken command of the Union Army.

General Robert E. Lee

Thomas J. (Stonewall) Jackson (1824–1863) was a brilliant field commander who had also graduated from West Point and served in the Mexican War. When the Civil War began, he was a professor at Virginia Military Institute. He was appointed a colonel of Virginia Volunteers when the war broke out, but became a hero and a general after he earned his nickname of "Stonewall" at the First Battle of Bull Run. He was also known as "Lee's right arm," because the two worked so well together. His best battle, Chancellorsville, was also his last. He was badly wounded and soon died after being shot by one of his own men who, in the darkness, mistook him for a Yankee.

James Longstreet (1821–1904) was also a West Point graduate and Mexican War veteran who chose to fight for the South. He proved to be a successful corps commander as long as he worked under Lee, but did not do nearly as well when he was on his own. He served faithfully and well, but was unpopular in the South after the war because of three things: (1) he argued with Lee over the wisdom of sending Pickett's men forward at Gettysburg, (2) he was right about the charge, and (3) he later became a Republican.

Jubal Early (1816–1894) was another West Point man and Mexican War veteran. He had a vengeful attitude that made him a terror in battle. He irritated Union troops so much that Grant ordered "veterans, militiamen, and everything that can be got to follow" and destroy him. Early reportedly said he liked pro-Union towns "because they burn so nicely."

James E. B. (Jeb) Stuart (1833–1864) had graduated from West Point and fought in Indian wars. He was the best known Confederate cavalryman and literally rode circles around Union armies. He practically forced the Union to improve its cavalry by making them look so bad.

Joseph Johnston (1807–1891) gave up a brigadier general's commission to serve the South. His arguments with President Davis kept him from being as successful as he might have been and caused him to be relieved of command at Atlanta. However, he was highly regarded as an opponent by General Sherman.

Name: _____ Date: _____

Activity: Skim and Scan

Directions: Use information from the reading selection to complete the activity.

		Who Am I?
1.	I was offered command of the Union Army, but refused it.	
2.	I was a successful commander when I worked with Lee, but didn't do well on my own.	
3.	I gave up a brigadier general's commission to serve the South.	
4.	I was known for being a terror in battle.	
5.	I wasn't popular in the South after the war, partly because I had argued with Lee at Gettysburg.	
6.	I was relieved of my command at Atlanta.	
7.	I was known as "Lee's right arm."	
8.	I was a brilliant field commander.	
9.	I had an amazing ability to think on the move and outguess my opponent.	
10.	I was the best known Confederate cavalryman.	

The Battle of New Orleans

For the Union to be successful, it was necessary to take control of the Mississippi River and cut the Confederacy in two. In the spring of 1862, the Union Navy began attacking Southern strongholds on the river. In April, John Pope captured the Confederate fortress at New Madrid, Missouri, called Island Number 10. On June 6, the Union fleet outgunned Confederate gunboats at Memphis, Tennessee; now, two-thirds of the river was in Union hands.

David Farragut

Farragut Attacks the Port of New Orleans

While those two victories were being won, a move designed to seize the rest of the river was taking shape. Flag Officer David Farragut was ordered to lead a fleet of 24 ships down the eastern seaboard and attack the port of New Orleans from the south.

Confederate officials had made Farragut's job very difficult. Forts Jackson and St. Philip stood opposite each other below New Orleans, both strongly built and well armed with heavy artillery. Between the two forts stretched a line of disabled ships, blocking the river to force attacking ships within easy range of the forts' guns.

Farragut's foster brother, Commander David Porter, proposed to solve the problem by sailing a small flotilla of ships, each armed with a 13-inch mortar, to a point just below the forts and shell them into rubble so the main fleet could pass safely. But after shelling Fort Jackson for a week, the fort still remained strong. Farragut decided on a more daring move. Under the cover of darkness, he would steam past the forts, smash through the barricade, and attack New Orleans.

During the night of April 23–24, two gunboats came up river and cut loose several ships blocking the channel. At 2 A.M., Farragut's fleet started past the forts, but the rising moon revealed the fleet, and the guns of the forts opened fire. The first Union vessel was hit 42 times. Farragut later said it felt like he was facing all the artillery on earth. His flagship, the *Hartford,* caught on fire, but the crew put out the flames. By dawn, nearly all of Farragut's ships were past the forts. At New Orleans, a makeshift squadron of eight ships came out to fight, but Farragut's guns sank six of them in minutes, the other two surrendered, and New Orleans fell without a shot being fired by the defending army.

The fall of New Orleans was a serious loss to the South, but the Mississippi River was not yet under Union control. Farragut continued upriver, taking Baton Rouge, Louisiana, and Natchez, Mississippi. But severing the Confederacy required taking the city of Vicksburg, Mississippi, located on a bluff 300 feet above the river, safely above Farragut's guns. It would require an army to take Vicksburg.

Military Governor of New Orleans Appointed

Farragut became a hero and America's first rear admiral. President Lincoln named Ben Butler military governor of New Orleans. He became very unpopular and was often referred to as "Beast Butler." He declared that slaves in the New Orleans area were free, and slaves flocked to the city from nearby plantations, further hurting the Southern war effort.

Name: _____ Date: _____

Activity: Map Skills

Directions: Use information from the reading selection to complete the map. Use your textbook or reference sources if you need help. Then study the map and answer the question.

1. Draw and label the Mississippi River.

2. Locate and label the cities of:
   New Orleans, Louisiana
   Baton Rouge, Louisiana
   Natchez, Mississippi
   Vicksburg, Mississippi

3. Why was capturing New Orleans and other Mississippi River cities so important to the Union?

The Border War

Early in the war as states chose sides, four states hung in the balance: Maryland, Delaware, Missouri, and Kentucky. All were slave states, but each had strong Unionist sentiments. They were important because their decisions could certainly affect the outcome of the war.

Delaware and Maryland

Delaware was never in doubt, but secessionists were strong in parts of Maryland, and Lincoln sent Union troops into the state to sway the public and the legislature. Fearing arrest if they voted for the South, Maryland's lawmakers passed resolutions supporting the Union.

Kentucky

Kentucky was so evenly divided that the legislature voted to proclaim neutrality and forbade either the United States or the Confederacy to operate within its borders. Both governments respected Kentucky's neutrality at first, but put troops just outside its borders to keep the other side from moving in. Union General Ulysses Grant sent several regiments of troops to Cairo, Illinois, on the Ohio River. Confederate General Leonidas Polk feared Grant would enter Kentucky to take the bluffs along the river, so he occupied the spot himself. Because the South had broken the state's neutrality, the Kentucky legislature invited Union troops in to drive the Rebels out. Grant moved in, occupying Paducah and Southland at the mouths of the Tennessee and Cumberland Rivers.

To hold Kentucky and protect Tennessee, General A.S. Johnston was ordered to direct Southern operations in the state. Union forces in Kentucky were divided between generals Carlos Buell and Henry Halleck. In January 1862, Confederate forces were defeated at Mill Springs and withdrew into Tennessee. Kentucky did not secede, but furnished 35,000 soldiers to the South.

Missouri

Missourians had argued over North-South issues. When the Civil War began, Governor Claiborne Jackson refused Lincoln's call for troops and tried to seize the U.S. federal arsenal at St. Louis. Captain Nathaniel Lyon, commander at the arsenal, shipped ammunition and 60,000 muskets to Illinois for safekeeping. In May 1861, he captured a pro-Confederate militia camp and marched his prisoners to St. Louis. That provoked rioting that killed 31 civilians and two soldiers.

Former Missouri governor Sterling Price recruited pro-Southern state guard units for the Confederacy. On August 10, 1861, Lyon attacked Price's camp at Wilson's Creek. Lyon was killed, and Price drove Union forces back toward Jefferson City. Guerilla warfare broke out all over the state. On September 20, Price defeated Union troops at Lexington, leaving southwest Missouri open to Southern occupation.

In November 1861, Lincoln appointed Henry Halleck as commander of the new Department of the Missouri, which included western Kentucky. By then, Price was under the command of Confederate General Earl Van Dorn, who planned to build a large army and capture St. Louis. Halleck sent General Samuel Curtis to attack Van Dorn at Pea Ridge, Arkansas. The Union victory there on March 7 and 8, 1862, kept Missouri in the Union, but did not prevent 30,000 Missourians from fighting in the Confederate Army.

> **Activity: Virtual Tour**
> Go online to <https://www.nps.gov/wicr/learn/photosmultimedia/virtual-tour-stop-1.htm> to view a virtual tour of the Wilson's Creek Battlefield in Missouri.

Name: _____ Date: _____

Activity: Key Details

Directions: Complete the graphic organizer with key details from the reading selection.

Delaware

Maryland

What did each of these Border States decide about secession?

Kentucky

Missouri

The Battle at Shiloh Church

After victories at Forts Henry and Donelson in Tennessee, the Union commanders were sure that the next battle would come whenever they chose. The Confederate commander, General Albert Johnston, withdrew to Corinth, Mississippi, and kept tabs on General Grant's activities just across the border in Tennessee. Reports of more Union troops arriving and General Don Carlos Buell's troops on the way were disturbing to Johnston and his second in command, recently arrived General P.G.T. Beauregard. One element was in their favor: the Union troops were making no effort to prepare defenses. With a force of 40,000 men, many of them raw recruits, Johnston decided to hit Grant before the Yankees united their forces.

An artist's drawing of the Battle of Shiloh Church

The Confederate march north was slow and far too noisy to suit Beauregard, who tried to persuade Johnston to call off the attack, but Johnston had made up his mind to go through with it.

On April 6, the Rebel forces hit troops of General Sherman and General Ben Prentiss, who were camped in an area around Shiloh Church, forcing them back. But in the thick woods and small clearings, it was impossible for the Southern forces to remain organized. Their strongest resistance came from Union troops hidden on a sunken road that was given the nickname of the "Hornet's Nest." Grant was seven miles away, at Savannah, Tennessee, when he heard the guns roaring that morning, and he took a steamboat to Pittsburg Landing, where he took charge of the situation. Prentiss was told to hold the Hornet's Nest at all cost.

That afternoon, Johnston received a leg wound he hardly noticed, but it had severed an artery, and he died soon afterward. Now, Beauregard was in command at a time when his troops were driving the Yankees back to the landing. However, Grant's defense was strengthened by a strong combination of artillery and gunboats. At 6 P.M., to the dismay of his troops, Beauregard called off operations for the day. It was a big mistake. During the night, Buell's 20,000 Yankees arrived, and the 20,000 reinforcements Beauregard expected from General Earl Van Dorn did not.

It rained hard that night, and the roar of Union cannons added to the misery of the Rebels. The Yankee attack began early in the morning, and Beauregard's troops were pushed back. Then they rallied and pushed the Yankees back to the Peach Orchard. When he learned Van Dorn had been held up in crossing the Mississippi, Beauregard began to withdraw. The Union soldiers were as worn out as his and made little effort to follow. Some attempt was made to pursue the Rebels on the 8th, but Confederate General Nathan Forrest's cavalry attacked and discouraged any further pursuit.

There were major failures in leadership on both sides; both generals (Beauregard and Grant) received much criticism from the press. For the troops, it was an unforgettable experience, as they had participated in the largest battle ever fought (to that time) on American soil. Casualties were high: 3,400 men dead and 16,000 wounded. Grant later said: "It was a high price to pay for a country church and steamboat dock."

Name: _____ Date: _____

Activity: Research

Directions: Research the life of one of the men listed in the box below. Use your research and information from the reading selection to complete the graphic organizer.

P.G.T. Beauregard	Don Carlos Buell	Nathan Forrest
Ulysses Grant	Albert Johnston	Ben Prentiss
William T. Sherman	Earl Van Dorn	

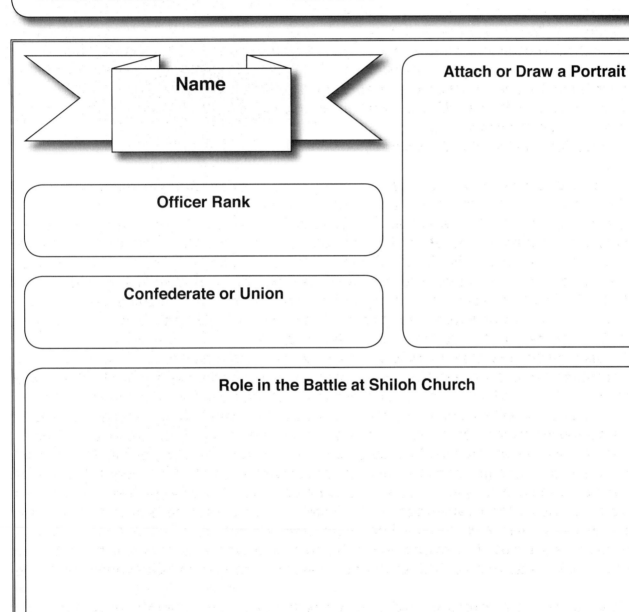

Name

Officer Rank

Confederate or Union

Attach or Draw a Portrait

Role in the Battle at Shiloh Church

Battle of Antietam

In September 1862, Confederate General Robert E. Lee began a campaign he hoped would take his army into Maryland and Pennsylvania. From there, he could strike at Philadelphia, Baltimore, or even Washington. If the drive was successful, the South might receive recognition by France and England and perhaps financial aid from one or both.

President Lincoln talks with General McClellan and other officers at Antietam, Maryland

McClellan Fears a Trap

On September 5, Lee's army pushed toward Frederick, Maryland. There, on September 9, he issued Special Order 191, dividing his army. He sent General Jackson to capture Harpers Ferry, while the main force moved toward Hagerstown. An officer carelessly wrapped the order around three cigars, and it was found by Union soldiers who took it to General McClellan on the 13th. With an army outnumbering Lee's by 36,000 men, and knowing that the opponent's army was split, most generals would have moved quickly to take advantage of the situation. But McClellan did not, partly because he feared this was a trap to pull him away from Washington so another Confederate Army could attack the capital.

Battle of Antietam

Finally, the next day, the two armies clashed at South Mountain, and the Confederates were pushed back. However, Jackson was successful in capturing Harpers Ferry on the 15th. When Lee learned of that victory later in the day, he decided to make his stand at Antietam Creek. With only 19,000 men on hand, the Potomac River at his back, and 40,000 men on the way to join him, Lee counted on McClellan to delay action, and he did. As McClellan planned the battle, his men would attack the Confederate left, then the right, and the reserves would be used to support either attack, or hit the Confederate center if Lee weakened it to support troops on either wing.

On September 17, action began with a fury when Union Generals Joe Hooker and Joe Mansfield's troops attacked the 12,000 Confederates under General John Hood hidden in a cornfield north of Sharpsburg. At first, the Yankees pushed the Rebels back, but then Hood's men retook the field, only to be met by fresh troops who forced them back again. In two hours of bitter fighting, Mansfield was killed, Hooker wounded, and the field littered with the dead and wounded.

The next focus of attention was the center where Union General Edwin "Bull Head" Sumner's troops charged toward Confederate General D.H. Hill's troops hidden in a sunken road. The Rebels held the road for three hours, and then Yankees overcame them; this piece of land would afterward be known as the "Bloody Lane." Now there was no Confederate center, but McClellan refused to send more troops into the area, fearing that this was a trap.

On the Confederate right, Union General Ambrose Burnside had been busy trying to move troops across a stone bridge (Burnside's Bridge) and finally was able to overcome General James Longstreet's resistance. At the moment when it appeared victory was at hand, Confederate General A.P. Hill's division arrived from Harpers Ferry and stopped Burnside in his tracks.

President Lincoln Fires General McClellan

It had been a long day with 4,100 dead and 18,500 more wounded in the most bloody day of the war. Lee expected McClellan to attack the next day, but when he did not, Lee crossed the Potomac. On November 5, 1862, Lincoln removed McClellan as Commander of the Army of the Potomac, and replaced him with General Burnside.

Name: _____ Date: _____

Activity: Fact and Opinion

Directions: Take a fact from the reading selection and rewrite it as an opinion. Remember, opinion statements sometimes contain signal words such as *best, most,* or *probably.* Opinion statements may also contain phrases such as *I believe, I think,* or *I feel.*

> ***Example***
> **Fact:** In September 1862, General Robert E. Lee began a campaign into Maryland and Pennsylvania.
>
> **Opinion:** I think the decision by General Robert E. Lee to begin a campaign into Maryland and Pennsylvania was a brilliant move.

Fact	Opinion

Medical Care in the Civil War

Nowhere was the lack of preparation for war more obvious than in the field of medicine. When the war began, the United States Army had 115 medical officers, 22 of whom resigned to join the Confederate Army. Politics plagued the U.S. Medical Department. Three surgeon generals were fired between 1861 and 1863; then Joseph Barnes took over the office and remained there until the end of the war. He saw the department expand to over 10,000 medical men. The South had no such political problems. Samuel Moore served as the Surgeon General of the Confederacy through the whole war. With resources very limited, he performed near-miracles. Unfortunately, when Richmond fell, the records of the Confederate medical department were destroyed, so little is known about how the department was organized.

Diseases and Camp Hygiene

Both medical departments faced enormous challenges. Neither the Union nor the Confederacy were experienced in handling large numbers of men in the field. Camp hygiene was so lacking that diseases spread through both armies. Of the 360,000 Union troops who died in war, 31 percent died of battle wounds and 69 percent of disease. Medical officers in both armies blamed health problems on spoiled food, polluted water, bad hygiene, infection from lice and fleas, and contagious diseases recruits brought to camp. The most common diseases were measles, mumps, and rheumatism. Cures for these and other diseases did not come until later.

Medical Care of Soldiers

Early in the war, wounded men were sheltered in schools, churches, barns, and even chicken houses near the battlefield. There were no organized field hospitals until the Union Army set one up at Shiloh in April 1862. There were no ambulances early in the war, and if a wounded man got to the surgeon, someone had to carry him there. Late in the war, horse-drawn ambulances were available to move the wounded.

Amputation was the usual cure for most wounded soldiers. Working quickly to prevent gangrene, surgeons cut off arms and legs, but then didn't bother to clean saws and other instruments between operations.

Medical System Emerges

Eventually, a system emerged featuring dressing stations on the battlefield where the injured man's wound was dressed. He was then sent to a hospital area in the rear. From there, he was either discharged or sent back to his unit. Women worked in these permanent hospitals. Female nurses were popular among patients, who longed for their gentle touch and soft words of comfort. A civilian organization, the U.S. Sanitary Commission, also supplied nurses to general hospitals. In the South, the Women's Relief Society sent volunteers to bathe, bandage, and comfort.

Shortage of Hospitals Addressed

Both sides had a shortage of hospitals. New ones were built, and other existing buildings (at colleges, warehouses, hotels, and railroad depots) were converted. The Chimborazo at Richmond was the largest during the war, and 76,000 men were treated there. The second largest was Lincoln, in Washington, which treated 46,000 men.

Activity: Research

To learn about a Civil War nurse, read *Clara Barton: The Founder of the American Red Cross* by Barbara A. Somervill.

Name: _____ Date: _____

Activity: Problem and Solution

Directions: Use the information in the reading selection to explain the solution to each problem with medical care during the Civil War.

No Ambulances

Solution:

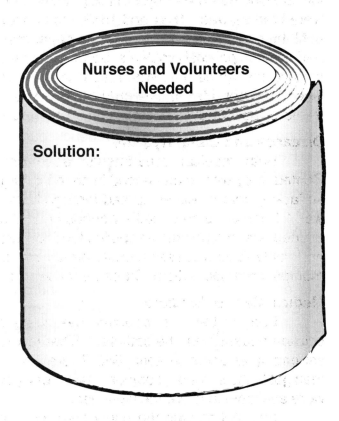

Nurses and Volunteers Needed

Solution:

No Organized Field Hospitals

Solution:

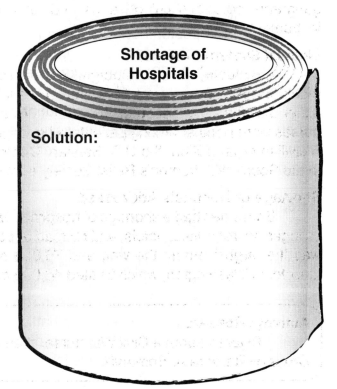

Shortage of Hospitals

Solution:

Battle of Fredericksburg

President Lincoln had tolerated General George B. McClellan's military leadership for over a year. He had ordered, pleaded, and coaxed McClellan to use the Army of the Potomac to its fullest and defeat General Robert E. Lee and the Confederate Army once and for all. Finally, after McClellan's failure to chase the Confederates after the battle at Antietam, Lincoln had had enough. In November 1862, McClellan was fired and replaced by Ambrose Burnside as major general of the Army of the Potomac.

Burnside's Plan to take Fredericksburg

The North demanded action, and General Burnside responded with a plan to take Fredericksburg, Virginia, on the Rappahannock River, then drive on to Richmond. The plan was simple and obvious, but it depended on taking Fredericksburg before Lee caught on to what was happening.

> **Did You Know?**
>
> The Battle of Fredericksburg involved more soldiers than any other battle during the Civil War.

The Confederate Army had been rebuilt since Antietam. Lee now had 72,000 men in two corps under the leadership of General Stonewall Jackson and General James Longstreet. The Union Army under Burnside's leadership consisted of 106,000 men led by three generals: Edwin Sumner, Joe Hooker, and William Franklin. Union troops began moving forward in mid-November and encamped across from Fredericksburg along the Rappahannock River. They were spotted by Confederate cavalry, and Lee sent Longstreet to Fredericksburg to keep an eye on them. Convinced a big battle was in the making, Lee's whole army went to Fredericksburg, eliminating the Union's element of surprise.

Burnside's plan depended on pontoon or floating bridges to cross the river, but red tape and bungling had sent them elsewhere. Burnside fumed until the pontoons were delivered two weeks later. Meanwhile, Confederate troops were busy building defenses and making plans.

A crescent-shaped line of hills ran around Fredericksburg. Lee's troops took up positions on Telegraph Hill, Marye's Heights, and Taylor's Hill. The Confederate calvary led by General James "Jeb" Stuart was posted between these hills and the river, and only one brigade was located in the town. At the foot of Marye's Heights was a sunken road, protected by a stone wall. General Longstreet placed 2,500 riflemen there. Lee waited for Burnside to make his crossing and walk into the trap.

Finally, General Burnside's pontoons arrived, and engineers went to work on assembling the bridges. Union troops began crossing the river on the bridges while nature pelted them with snow, sleet, and freezing winds. On December 13, a heavy fog lifted at midmorning and Burnside's long-delayed attack began.

Defeat at Fredericksburg

Union General George Meade struck General Jackson's position south of town, but was stopped by Confederate troops. In town, Generals Sumner and Hooker ordered Union troops to join the fight at Marye's Heights. The soldiers marched forward in parade formation and were mowed down by Confederate artillery positioned on the hills overlooking Fredericksburg. Seven attempts were made to reach the sunken road, and the bodies continued to pile up in front of the wall. Burnside wanted to continue the battle, but his officers argued strongly against it, and they prevailed. The Southern generals were disappointed when they found the Yankees had pulled back. Burnside's failure cost him his job, and 12,700 of his men lost their lives or were severely wounded.

Name: _____ Date: _____

Activity: Making Inferences

An **inference** is a conclusion a reader makes based on evidence and reasoning rather than from explicit statements in the reading selection.

Directions: Think about what you learned from the reading selection and what you already know. Then complete the graphic organizer. Support your answer with details and examples.

How did the geography of Fredericksburg contribute to the defeat of the Union Army?

Rappahannock River	Crescent-shaped Line of Hills	Sunken Road

The Draft Is Imposed: North and South

After the first rush to join the army at the beginning of the Civil War, there was a noticeable drop in enlistments in both the North and the South. This could be partly blamed on marching and drilling, poor food, uncomfortable tents, and sergeants and officers yelling at recruits. Stories of battles, death, and wounds also discouraged the faint-hearted. If men did not choose to fight, new means had to be found to fill the ranks of the army and protect the nation.

Recruiting office in New York

The South was first to adopt the draft. In April 1862, the draft required military service of men from ages 18 to 35. Five months later, the upper age was set at 45, and in 1864, the draft included those from 17 to 50. There were exceptions. Certain professions and occupations were excluded, a man could hire a substitute, and one exemption would be granted to every master or overseer of every 20 slaves. Since teachers and druggists were exempt, many men entered those professions. In some parts of the South, especially mountain regions, it required great effort to catch draft dodgers, who saw no advantage in fighting to preserve slavery for the rich. By 1863, ads offering $6,000 for an acceptable substitute appeared in newspapers. Because of desertions and losses to disease, the South's manpower supply was so reduced that General Patrick Cleburne suggested using slaves in the army. General Lee lent his support to that idea in January 1865; the bill passed in March, but the war ended before slaves fought for the Confederate States of America.

The Union's draft law was as unpopular as the South's. The Enrollment Act passed in March 1863 included able-bodied men between 20–45 years of age for service not to exceed three years. There were exemptions allowed, including some professions, those who hired substitutes, or those who paid the government $300. In both the North and South, those subject to the draft complained this was a "rich man's war and a poor man's fight."

Communities reacted differently to the draft. A riot began in New York City that lasted from July 13–17, 1863. The hoodlum element in the city, drunk and savage, attacked black people on the streets, looted stores, and shoved aside anyone trying to stop them. The mayor asked the governor for help, and on the second day of the riot, Governor Horatio Seymour arrived. Addressing the mob as "My friends," he tried to quiet them by saying an aide had been sent to President Lincoln urging him to call off the draft.

Many Northern counties faced a problem. They did not want to draft men; that made the county look unpatriotic and turned voters against the local officials. Their problem was solved by a "bounty broker," who promised county officials he could find enough men to fill the quota. Some brokers resorted to trickery to find enough men. A broker found most recruits in bars; after getting the men drunk, the broker turned them over to a recruiting sergeant. Brokers also found underage boys to fill the draft quota. Brokers had a woman who claimed she was the boy's mother sign his enlistment papers. Brokers took old men, put black shoe polish on their hair, and claimed they were much younger. Very few qualified men were brought into the army by brokers.

Name: _____ Date: _____

Activity: Cause and Effect

Directions: Complete the graphic organizer using information from the reading selection.

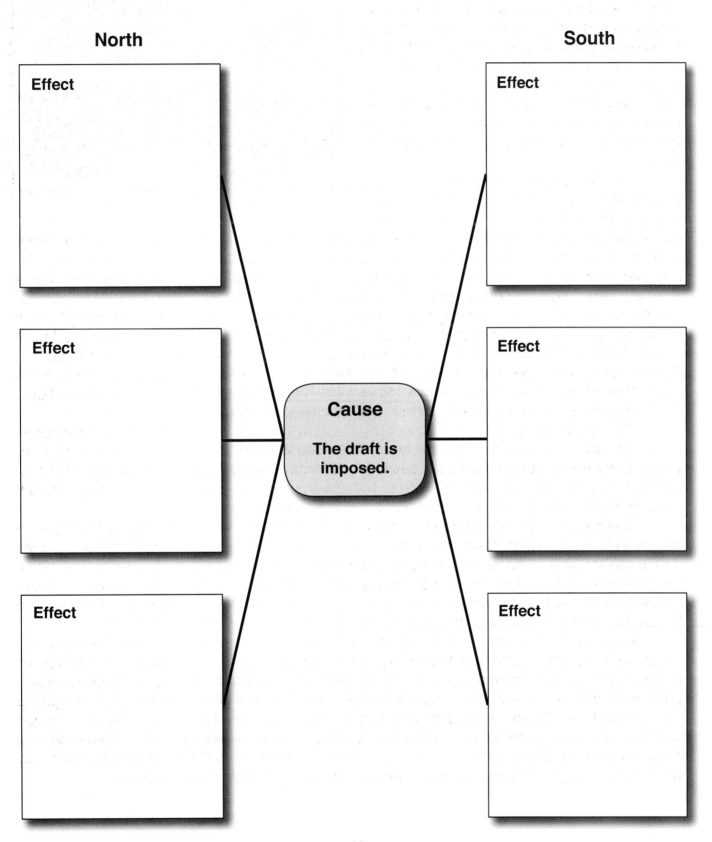

North   **South**

Effect

Effect

Effect

Effect

Effect

Effect

Cause

The draft is imposed.

Congress Passes New Legislation

When one thinks about the Civil War, one may think about generals and battles, but seldom of Congress. The reason is that President Lincoln made the decision to go to war himself. Congress would not be in session until July 1861. By then, Lincoln had called up 75,000 volunteers, blockaded the southern coastline, and borrowed money to pay the costs. When Congress finally met, Lincoln asked their approval for what had already been done. They had little choice except to go along with him. Lincoln had made it clear that when it came to

Congress passed the Homestead Act of 1862, which gave homesteaders 160 acres of government prairie land.

the war, he was the one in charge. Congress was reluctant to let him have so much power and kept an eagle eye on him.

Radical Republicans thought President Lincoln was too easy on the South. They pushed to create the Joint Committee on the Conduct of the War, which investigated generals and often embarrassed Lincoln. Most Democrats said he was not doing enough to make peace. One of these, Representative Clement Vallandigham, said the war was "wicked, cruel and unnecessary." He was arrested by General Burnside for that remark. With the war going badly, most in Congress willingly let President Lincoln take over and take the blame.

Republicans in Congress remembered how Southern Democrats had always blocked their proposals to raise the tariff (taxes on imports), give government land to farmers (homesteaders), and build a railroad from the North to California. With Republicans in control of the White House and Congress, the time was right for them to fulfill the campaign promises of the 1860 Republican Party platform (policies).

The first change was to increase taxes. The Federal government had never spent money as quickly as it was now, so Congress passed the Morrill Tariff in 1861. This was an excise tax, a special tax on the sale of some luxuries. They also added an income tax. With government expenses far higher than income, the government began selling bonds. They were still so short on cash that the "greenback" was issued. This paper money was used to pay debts, but it was backed only by faith in the government. If battles were being lost, greenback value dropped. When battles were won, the value went up. Debate over greenbacks went on for years.

In May 1862, Congress passed the Homestead Act offering free land to homesteaders to encourage settlement of western territory. The law allowed any citizen or person intending to become a citizen to settle on 160 acres of government land. After living there five years, the land would be the homesteader's to keep.

Congress also passed the Pacific Railroad Act in 1862. The law chartered two railroad companies, the Central Pacific and the Union Pacific, with the job of building a transcontinental railroad that would link the United States from east to west. In 1864, Congress chartered the Northern Pacific to be built from Lake Superior to Portland, Oregon. When the war ended and thousands of unemployed veterans were eager to find work, construction moved forward quickly. In 1869, the Central Pacific and Union Pacific Railroads met at Promontory Point, Utah, making transportation of people and goods from the Atlantic to the Pacific faster and easier.

Name: _____ Date: _____

Activity: Problem and Solution

Directions: Complete the graphic organizer using information from the reading selection. Support your answers with examples and details.

Problem #1

Congress wanted to raise taxes to increase revenue.

Solution

Problem #2

Congress wanted to settle the western territory.

Solution

Problem #3

Congress wanted to make transportation from the Atlantic to the Pacific faster and easier.

Solution

Civilians and the War Effort

It is in the nature of modern warfare that civilians become involved, whether they want to or not. Wilmer McLean, a farmer at Bull Run in Virginia, became part of the Civil War when the first battle of the war was fought on his land. He had enough of that and moved his family to Appomattox. Others like him saw armies moving past their farms and through their towns and hoped no one would stop long enough to have a battle or loot a house. Many came out to cheer their troops and brought buckets of cool water. Volunteers were going to play a big part in the war.

In 1862, the studio of Matthew Brady took this portrait of Confederate spy Rose O'Neal Greenhow and her daughter "Little Rose" in Washington, D.C., at the Old Capitol Prison.

Women Spies

Some civilians acted as spies. The Confederate spy Rose Greenhow was acquainted with many government officials, and the information she collected was used to help General Beauregard at Bull Run. Belle Boyd became the most famous Confederate spy, sending information and medicine to help General Stonewall Jackson's army. Keeping a watchful eye on Confederates was the Pinkerton Detective Agency's assignment during the war. Elizabeth Van Lew and her former slave, Mary Bowser, provided useful information for the Union Army from their home in Richmond, Virginia. Many who were never known kept leaders informed on the movement of enemy armies.

Women Volunteers

Nurses known as "angels of the battlefield" served during the Civil War. President Lincoln gave Dorothea Dix the title of Superintendent of U.S. Army Nurses, and even though she had faults in her methods of doing her job, she was successful in enlisting public support. She asked the public for canned goods and night shirts, and more were given than the army needed. Clara Barton, later famous as head of the American Red Cross, served as a battlefield nurse during the war and held the title of Superintendent of Nurses for the Army of the James. Mary Bickerdyke became a hero to many wounded enlisted men and did much to improve the quality of their care. Dr. Mary Walker became an assistant surgeon for the army, and even though she was a civilian, she was awarded the Congressional Medal of Honor.

Voluntary Groups

Voluntary organizations and churches organized to meet special needs. The U.S. Sanitary Commission raised money through "Sanitary Fairs" for a program to supply food, clothing, bandages, and medicine for the troops. The YMCA and Protestant ministers formed the Christian Commission to provide nursing care, blankets, and medicine to wounded soldiers. The Catholic Sisters of Charity supplied nurses to army hospitals. Many individuals, churches, and communities helped traveling soldiers with a place to stop, rest, and talk. Untold hours of work by women wrapping bandages and preparing jelly or meals for the troops helped provide some reminder of home to men far away from loved ones.

The unsung heroes were those women and children who plowed the land, milked the cows, and repaired the fences, so that fathers, husbands, and sons could go into the army and serve their nation with a clear conscience.

Name: _____ Date: _____

Activity: Summarizing

Directions: Complete the graphic organizer using information from the reading selection.

Main Idea

Volunteers played
an important role
in the Civil War.

Women Spies

Voluntary Groups

Women Volunteers

Civil Rights in the North During the War

Imagine that you are walking down the street one day, and a policeman grabs you and takes you to jail. No one tells you why you are being held, and the police never take your case to court. You could sit there for years, unless you were protected by the writ of *habeas corpus*, which gives you the right to go to court and have the charges against you read. Article 1, Section 9 of the Constitution guarantees citizens this right except "in cases of rebellion or invasion the public safety may require it."

Writ of *Habeas Corpus* Suspended

In April 1861, troops marching through Baltimore were attacked by mobs throwing bricks and stones. In that fight, twelve civilians and four soldiers were killed. In retaliation, many Maryland railroad bridges were burned and telegraph lines cut by Southern sympathizers, causing Washington to be cut off from the rest of the North.

President Lincoln decided the emergency required quick action. He ordered General Winfield Scott to suspend the writ of *habeas corpus* in the area from Washington, D.C., to Philadelphia. This action gave the military the right to arrest, imprison, and hold civilians without a trial.

John Merryman was one of the men accused of burning bridges and cutting telegraph lines in Maryland. He was arrested and taken to Fort McHenry. His lawyer claimed Merryman had a right to go to court and take his appeal to the circuit court. The chief judge of the circuit was Roger Taney, the U.S. Supreme Court's chief justice. He issued a writ of *habeas corpus*, but the fort's commander refused to bring Merryman to court. Taney wrote that President Lincoln had no authority to suspend the writ, since Article 1 deals with powers of Congress, not the president; Taney claimed the Constitution did not permit a citizen to be held without a trial. Seven weeks later, Merryman was released. Merryman was to be tried in the circuit court, but the case was never brought to court because the government knew no Maryland jury would convict him.

Newspapers and Mail

If a newspaper was believed to be disloyal, the army might arrest the editor and hold him for a few days. Another method was to refuse to allow the papers to be mailed. The postmaster-general justified the policy by saying that a newspaper could not criticize the government and the Union and then claim their protection. The policy also stated mail could not be used for the government's destruction.

Religious Objectors

Quakers were opposed to war, but all except one had paid $300 to the government or hired a substitute. The exception was Cyrus Pringle, who refused to do either of those, but when drafted, he refused to obey any orders. His situation came to President Lincoln's attention, and he ordered the man sent home. In 1864, the War Department made a policy that religious objectors were to be used in hospitals, or take care of freedmen, or pay $300 for the care of sick and wounded soldiers.

Military Courts Try Civilians

Lambdin P. Milligan, a civilian, was arrested in 1864 for disloyalty to the Union. Even though he was a civilian, he was tried by a military court and sentenced to be hanged. He appealed to the Supreme Court, which ruled in 1866 that the president could not try civilians in military courts in areas where regular courts were operating.

Name: _____ Date: _____

Activity: Recalling Information

Directions: Complete the graphic organizer using information from the reading selection.

Question 1:

What was the effect of Lincoln suspending the writ of *habeas corpus* in 1861?

Answer:

_____

_____

_____

_____

_____

Question 2:

After 1864, how did the Union Army handle religious objectors?

Answer:

_____

_____

_____

_____

_____

Question 3:

How did the government handle disloyal newspapers during the Civil War?

Answer:

_____

_____

_____

_____

_____

Question 4:

What was the Supreme Court's decision in the case of Lambdin P. Milligan?

Answer:

_____

_____

_____

_____

_____

The Emancipation Proclamation

Black Union soldiers at Fort Corcoran near Washington, D.C.

One of the most troubling questions of the Civil War was whether slaves should be emancipated (freed), and, if so, when it should be done. In the early stages of the war, Congress said that the purpose of the war was to save the Union, not end slavery. That view was very close to the one held by President Lincoln. In August 1862, Lincoln answered criticism from Horace Greeley, editor of the *New York Tribune*. Lincoln replied that regardless of his personal wish that slavery end, "My paramount object in this struggle is to save the Union, and is not either to save or to destroy slavery." Lincoln's problem was that loyal Border States like Missouri, Kentucky, and Maryland still had slaves; he could not risk stirring up more opposition in those states.

Free Colony on the Island of Île à Vache

Northern opinion at the time was as divided as it could possibly be. The old abolitionists were sure that freeing slaves was right. Others supported the idea of colonization, the freeing of slaves, but sending them to Africa or Central America. Freedmen opposed this idea, and one, Robert Purvis, bluntly told Lincoln: "Sir, this is our country as much as it is yours, and we will not leave it." Despite protests from free blacks and abolitionists, President Lincoln tried to establish a colony on Île à Vache, a Caribbean island off the coast of Haiti. His plan was a miserable failure, and after many of the black "colonists" became ill, the survivors were brought back to America.

Emancipation Proclamation

There were some legal questions about freeing slaves in loyal states. Amendment V of the Constitution says that private property cannot be taken without just compensation. President Lincoln offered a deal to Border State leaders: free your slaves, and the government will pay $400 for each one. They turned him down flat. If he could not persuade loyal Border States to free slaves, Lincoln could justify freeing Confederate slaves as a war measure. On January 1, 1863, Lincoln signed the Emancipation Proclamation, freeing slaves in those states still at war with the Union. It was not until 1865 and the 13th Amendment that all slavery in the United States was made a thing of the past.

Black Soldiers in the Union Army

The Emancipation Proclamation raised another question. Should black men be enlisted in the army? Black leaders like Frederick Douglass pointed out that General Ben Butler was already using escaped slaves at Fortress Monroe to build defenses. They were given a shovel and pick for digging, a red shirt to wear, and a pistol for their belt. Lincoln opposed the idea. He believed the enlistment of black soldiers would cause the Border States to become even a greater obstacle to the Union cause. However, by early 1863, President Lincoln was ready to accept black men into the Union Army. The Bureau of Colored Troops was created, and General Lorenzo Thomas was sent to the Mississippi Valley to recruit blacks. He was able to enlist 76,000 black soldiers.

Black regiments were led by white officers, with less than 100 black men ever becoming officers. The enthusiasm of black regiments ran high, though in battle they often suffered high casualties. In May 1863, black troops drove off a Confederate attack at Milliken's Bend, Mississippi. That July, the 54th Massachusetts Infantry, one of the first official black regiments, proved itself as it attempted to take Fort Wagner, South Carolina. Black soldiers could take pride in helping to make freedom a reality for those still held as slaves.

Name: _____ Date: _____

Activity: Recalling Information

Directions: Complete the graphic organizer using information from the reading selection.

Position	**Civil War Issue**	**Position**
President Lincoln	Purpose of the War	Congress
President Lincoln	Freeing Slaves	Leaders of the Border States
President Lincoln	Black Soldiers	Frederick Douglass

Battle of Chancellorsville

After General Burnside's crushing defeat at Fredericksburg in 1862, President Lincoln again searched for a general to lead the Army of the Potomac. In January 1863, he chose General Joseph Hooker for the job, but doubted that he had the right man. He warned Hooker that the army had a defeatist spirit, and that would be a problem. He told Hooker not to be rash, but "with energy and sleepless vigilance go forward and give us victories."

General Thomas "Stonewall" Jackson

Confederate and Union Armies

The Confederate Army led by General Robert E. Lee, on the other hand, had a confidence that ignored its ragged and hungry appearance. Despite the cold, the men enjoyed large snowball fights and waited for the Yankees to come back for another licking.

Hooker worked hard at rebuilding his army's confidence. When President Lincoln came out to see the army, he assured the president they were the "finest army on the planet" and would drive his way through to Richmond, Virginia. Such boasting bothered Lincoln, who felt that defeating the enemy in battle was more important than capturing the Confederate's capital.

Battle of Chancellorsville

From April 30 to May 6, 1863, during the Battle of Chancellorsville, General Hooker had a chance to make good on his boast. Hooker began the battle well, confusing the Confederates by moving at different points at the same time. The area involved was between Fredericksburg and Kelly's Ford, which crossed the Rappahannock River near the village of Chancellorsville, a distance of about 15 miles. Union Army General Sedgwick was to hold General Lee and his troops at Fredericksburg. Hooker would take 40,000 Union soldiers west to Kelly's Ford. When Sedgwick's soldiers put pontoons across the river but made no effort to cross, Lee knew that this was a trick, and the main attack would be elsewhere. Cavalry reports of a large movement westward meant he should shift his troops in that direction. Lee left Confederate General Jubal Early at Fredericksburg with 10,000 men and took 50,000 soldiers with him.

On May 1, 1863, advanced units of the armies clashed. Hooker pulled back his Union Army and began building defenses. After Confederate General Jeb Stuart's cavalry reported that Hooker's right flank (side) was unsupported, Lee and General "Stonewall" Jackson drew up plans for a bold attack. Jackson was to take 26,000 men and move in front of the Union line around to its right flank. He would be aided by the thick undergrowth, but if he were attacked while on the move or if Lee's 17,000 men were hit by Hooker's Union troops, it would become a Confederate disaster.

Hooker's pickets observed Jackson and his Rebel troops on the road, but Hooker paid no attention to the reports. At 6 P.M. on May 2, Jackson struck the west end of the Union line, driving the Yankees back in great confusion. That night, Jackson went out to observe the enemy positions in preparation for a night attack. One of his men, mistaking him for a Union solder, fired and wounded him. Jackson would later die from the wound. Stuart took command of Jackson's men and continued the attack. Hooker had more troops and the split in Confederate forces gave him the advantage, but the only aggressive action he took was to send Sedgwick against Early. After Early and his Confederate troops were pushed back, the army went to support Lee's troops and in turn drove Sedgwick and the Union troops back. Hooker then withdrew the Union Army across the river, another humiliation for the "finest army on the planet" and for Lincoln.

Name: _____ Date: _____

Activity: Making Inferences

> An **inference** is a conclusion a reader makes based on evidence and reasoning rather than from explicit statements in the reading selection.

Directions: Think about what you have learned from the reading selection and what you already know. Then answer the questions below. Support your answer with details and examples.

1. Why do you think the morale of the Confederate Army was higher than that of the men in the Army of the Potomac?

2. Why do you think President Lincoln felt that General Hooker might not be the right man to lead the Army of the Potomac?

Victory at Vicksburg

Vicksburg, the last Confederate stronghold on the Mississippi River, sat comfortably on a high bluff overlooking the river and the marshy lowlands to the west. With 10 miles of defenses to its north and 40 miles to its south, Vicksburg's guns controlled the river, which made a large U-shaped bend just before it passed the guns guarding the city. After other river cities had fallen, only Vicksburg connected Texas, Arkansas, and Louisiana with the rest of the Confederacy. In 1862, Union naval commander David Farragut led two attacks against this Confederate defense and failed. General Ulysses S. Grant wanted to try, and Union Army commander Henry Wager Halleck gave in: "Fight the enemy where you please."

Union Troops Beat Back

General Grant's efforts got off to a poor start. His first move was on December 26, 1862. He led a 40,000-man army southward down the Mississippi Central Railroad, and General William T. Sherman, with 32,000 Union soldiers, moved by boat down the river. Grant's efforts were halted when General Earl Van Dorn's Confederate cavalry hit his main supply base at Holly Springs, Mississippi, and General Nathan Bedford Forrest's cavalry tore up 60 miles of track behind him in Tennessee. Grant had to withdraw, but could not get word to Sherman, whose army was soon beaten back at Chickasaw Bluffs.

Grant made several attempts during the winter of 1863 to find a way to bypass the Vicksburg guns. Nothing worked. Although Grant had little hope the attempts would succeed, he thought it was better to try than for his men to be idle.

In March 1863, Grant moved south by land on the west side of the river to a point below Vicksburg. On April 16, 1863, Rear Admiral Porter, now in charge of the river fleet, came down the Mississippi under fire from Confederate guns on the bluffs of Vicksburg, to ferry Grant's troops across the river. Porter's fleet was spotted and shore guns blasted away; all the boats were hit, but only one was sunk. Porter's second fleet was not as lucky; it lost six barges and a transport.

Grant Takes Vicksburg

To keep John Pemberton, the Confederate Army commander at Vicksburg, from bothering his crossing, Grant had two diversions planned. Sherman's troops moved toward Chickasaw Bluffs, and Union General Grierson's cavalry hit a railroad used to supply Vicksburg from the east. When his troops made it across the river, Grant headed toward the state capital of Jackson, Mississippi. After defeating Confederate troops under the command of General Joseph Johnston, Grant moved westward straight toward Vicksburg. The Confederate defenses were well prepared, and after Union attempts failed to break through them, Grant's troops besieged the city on May 25, 1863.

In the long siege, soldiers of the two armies became acquainted with each other. They traded bread for tobacco one day, and the next, tried to kill each other. Conditions inside the city became primitive. Shelling made it unsafe to live in houses, so the citizens dug caves in the bluffs for shelter. Food was in short supply, so people ate horses, mules, dogs, cats, and muskrats. Due to the low food supply and the possibility that Union forces would make a strong attack, Confederate General Pemberton surrendered Vicksburg on July 4, 1863. He arranged with Grant for his troops to be paroled, rather than sent to a prison camp. Grant captured 31,600 soldiers, 172 cannons, 60,000 muskets, and a large supply of ammunition. But as great as his achievement was, the nations' eyes were focused on Gettysburg that day.

Name: _____ Date: _____

Activity: Timeline

Directions: Complete the graphic organizer using information from the reading selection. Fill in the event for each date on the timeline.

Grant at Vicksburg

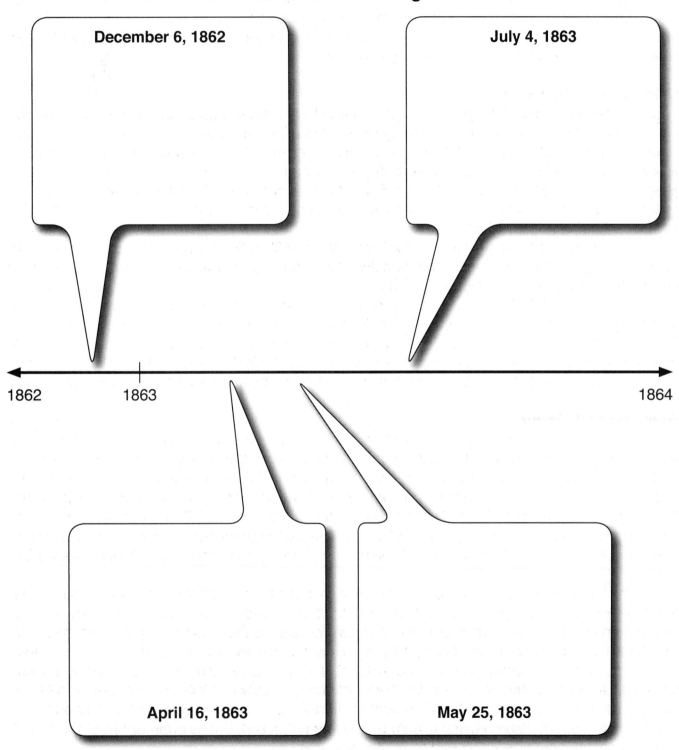

Events Leading Up to the Battle of Gettysburg

The victorious Army of Northern Virginia had demonstrated its skill at Chancellorsville, and the spirits of the men couldn't have been higher. Western Confederate armies were in trouble, however. General Grant had moved south of Vicksburg, captured Jackson, and was closing in on Vicksburg, Mississippi, from the east. Confederate General Longstreet wanted to go to Tennessee and help General Bragg in the Chattanooga area, but General Lee had a different plan: invade Pennsylvania. This could accomplish several things: encourage Peace Democrats, force Union troops in Tennessee and Mississippi to be pulled east, and allow his army to live off food and supplies taken from the Yankees for a change.

*General
George Meade*

Lee Reorganizes the Confederate Army

After General Jackson's death, Lee reorganized his army into three corps instead of two. Commanders were now James Longstreet, Richard Ewell, and A.P. Hill. When the army moved, it was important that Union General Joseph Hooker not know where they were or where they were going. In June of 1863, Hooker guessed the Confederates were moving, and his cavalry met the Confederate cavalry under General J.E.B. Stuart in the Battle of Brandy Station, the largest cavalry battle of the war. For the first time, Union cavalry performed as well as the Rebels, and Stuart received much public criticism. More importantly, Hooker now knew where Lee was. Ewell had a much easier time than Stuart in defeating Union troops led by General Milroy at Winchester.

President Lincoln Replaces General Hooker

By mid-June, the Rebels were in Pennsylvania, visiting farmers, merchants, and stores, paying for what they took in Confederate money. On June 23, Stuart's Confederate cavalry headed east to harass the Yankees, destroy their supplies, and gather information. Stuart's instructions were vague, but his trip took far too long, and Lee lost the "eyes of his army." Lee's army spread over a large area 100 miles west to east and 40 miles north to south. Hooker suggested to President Lincoln that this was an ideal time to attack Richmond; the president told him that Lee's army was more important to defeat than seizing the Confederate capital. Lincoln had lost confidence in Hooker and decided it was time to change commanders.

The responsibility of stopping Lee's advance fell to General George Meade. Unlike General Joseph Hooker, who wanted to lead the Army of the Potomac, Meade was content to let someone else lead. However, on June 28, 1863, Meade was told to assume command. Meade was an able officer, but his hot temper made him unpopular, and his troops described him as a "goggle-eyed snapping turtle."

Troops Gather at Gettysburg

Lee hoped to avoid any major battle until his army was reunited, so when he learned on June 28, 1863, that the Yankees were north of the Potomac River, he sent an order for all Confederate units to gather near Gettysburg. General A.P. Hill, already near Gettysburg, decided to visit the town. His soldiers needed shoes and he planned to seize the shoes that were reportedly stored in the town. Arriving on July 1, he found that General John Buford's Union cavalry was already there. Then General John Reynolds arrived with more Union troops. Soon, Ewell arrived with Confederate soldiers to support Hill. Over the next three days, one of the world's most important battles took place as both sides fought for the hills near this quiet town.

Name: _____ Date: _____

Activity: Skim and Scan

Directions: List the names of Union and Confederate generals in the graphic organizer. Then make each statement true by circling the correct word inside the parentheses.

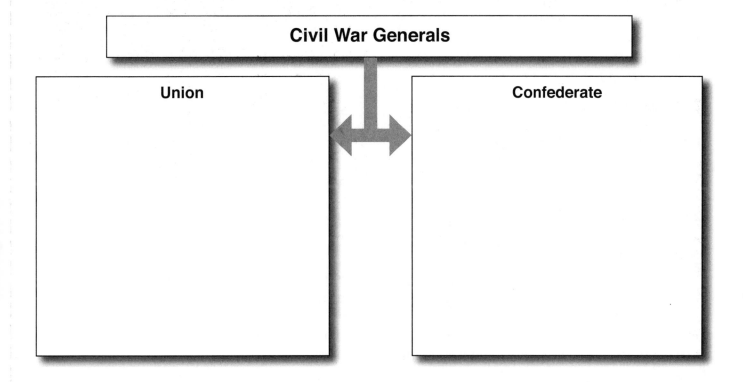

Statements

1. Lincoln had lost confidence in General (**Hooker's** / **Meade's**) ability to lead the Army of the Potomac and decided it was time to change commanders.

2. In June of 1863, Union troops met Confederate soldiers at the Battle of Brandy Station, resulting in the largest (**cavalry** / **naval**) battle of the war.

3. On June 28, 1863, after learning that the Yankees were north of the Potomac, General (**Lee** / **Reynolds**) sent out an order for all Confederate units to gather near Gettysburg.

4. (**Confederate** / **Union**) General Hill went to Gettysburg to seize shoes that were reportedly being stored in the town.

Battle of Gettysburg

While no one had selected an area near Gettysburg, Pennsylvania, as the place to fight the battle of the century, once there, Robert E. Lee, commander of the Confederate Army, decided that General George Meade and the Union forces must be engaged there. The Battle of Gettysburg took place over a three-day period in July of 1863. Lee along with his officers, Longstreet, Ewell, and Pickett, made several mistakes that led to the Union victory at Gettysburg.

Gateway of Gettysburg Cemetery, July 1863

Cemetery Hill and Seminary Ridge

On July 1, 1863, the first day of the battle, the two armies met in the fields west of Gettysburg. The Confederate Army outnumbered the Union Army and after a full day of fighting, the Union Army retreated to Cemetery Hill. Lee ordered Ewell to follow and attack the fleeing army. Ewell held back and did not attack. This provided the Union Army with a chance to regroup and take up defensive positions on the hill.

When General Meade arrived on July 2, he found the Union Army dug in on top of Cemetery Hill and Cemetery Ridge. Unknown to Lee, the 94,000 Union troops now outnumbered the 72,000 Confederate troops.

General Lee studied the Union troops from his position on Seminary Ridge, trying to find a weakness. He finally decided a weakness might be in the Union's left flank (side). He ordered Longstreet to immediately attack. But Longstreet failed to get his troops in position in time to take advantage of the weakness. The fighting was fierce, and both sides suffered heavy causalities. It was all in vain, however, as Union troops managed to hold them back.

Pickett's Charge

Lee's army had suffered heavy losses, but had also inflicted them. He felt that with one grand rush, he might be able to break the Union's spirit. That task was assigned to the troops of General George Pickett. Longstreet was strongly opposed to this move, but gave up when he saw Lee had made up his mind. The first gun duel of July 3 was on the eastern flank of the line, where Ewell's troops were driven off Culp's Hill. Then there was a stillness in the hot air, as each army prepared for the coming storm.

It struck at 1:00 P.M. as 140 Confederate cannons opened fire and 118 Union cannons responded. The artillery went at each other for two hours. Running low on ammunition, Pickett's 10,500 Confederate soldiers formed in three ranks as if on parade. At 3:10 P.M., they moved forward at 110 paces a minute across a mile of open ground. The Union fired everything available at them, but the Rebel wave kept coming, and some reached the Yankee line before being killed or captured. It had been a heroic effort, but a dismal failure. As the survivors returned, Lee met them and tried to encourage them. When Pickett saw Lee, he was told to move his division behind the woods; Pickett replied: "General Lee, I have no division."

Confederate Troops Retreat

Lee, Longstreet, and others in the high command prepared for Meade to attack their weakened troops, but Meade felt his men were too tired. On July 4, the Confederates began to withdraw, but heavy rains prevented crossing the Potomac until July 13. Lincoln was very disappointed in Meade's lack of movement after the battle. Casualties on both sides totaled at least 47,000 men.

Name: _____ Date: _____

Activity: Making Inferences

An **inference** is a conclusion a reader makes based on evidence and reasoning rather than from explicit statements in the reading selection.

Directions: Think about what you learned from the reading selection and what you already know. Then complete the graphic organizer. Support your answers with details and examples.

Mistakes Made at Gettysburg by the Confederates

Day 1

Day 2

Day 3

General Grant Takes Charge

General Ulysses S. Grant at his headquarters in Cold Harbor, Virginia

By 1864, many Union generals important in the beginning of the war were gone; they had failed to win battles and now were either out of the army or moved to less important positions. Irvin McDowell, who lost at Bull Run, now led the Army of the Pacific. George McClellan went home after Antietam to wait for new orders; he never received them. John Pope, loser at Second Bull Run, was sent to work out problems with the Sioux Indians. Ambrose Burnside, defeated at Fredericksburg, was now working under General Grant. Joe Hooker, after Chancellorsville, served in battles like Chickamauga, Chattanooga, and Lookout Mountain. No matter how well he did, Hooker never received the credit from Grant that was given to William T. Sherman.

Generals Provide Solutions

No other president faced the problems Abraham Lincoln did in raising and supplying an army anywhere near the size of the Union Army. No president had ever dealt with such complex military strategy questions. A president needs good help in such times. The quartermaster general, Montgomery Meigs, did an excellent job of supplying the troops with clothing, shoes, and food. No army had ever eaten as well. Many mistakes were made at first, but President Lincoln learned quickly. In this, he had help from General Henry Halleck, whose main talent was explaining military problems and strategies to an army largely composed of civilian volunteers.

A New Breed of Generals

When Ulysses Grant was named general-in-chief, it was a title well deserved. However, his friend William T. Sherman warned him against the political intrigue around Washington and advised that he set up headquarters elsewhere. The eastern soldiers were prepared to hate him, but Grant was so unassuming that he changed many of their minds. One officer saw only three emotions in him: "deep thought, extreme determination, and great simplicity and calmness." Critics were also there, pointing out his reputation for drinking, his poor grammar, and his inability to march in step.

Like Grant, Sherman had been unsuccessful in civilian life, but war had changed him. When it began, he wanted to play it by the old rules: no stealing, robbery, or pillaging. However, by 1864, he wrote Halleck: "We are not only fighting hostile armies, but a hostile people, and must make old and young, rich and poor, feel the hard hand of war." With the war nearly won, his former attitude returned, and he became more benevolent.

Other generals in the Union Army provided a wide variety of skills and personalities. If one preferred the colorful, George Custer was the man. Last in his class at West Point in 1861, he later became a major general in the U.S. Volunteers in 1865. Ben Butler was controversial but was protected from being punished for his mistakes because he was a Democrat, and Lincoln needed support for the war from the opposition party. Serving in the Union Army was a future road to the presidency. In addition to Grant, Rutherford B. Hayes, James Garfield, Chester Arthur, and Benjamin Harrison were generals; William McKinley was a major.

Name: _____ Date: _____

Activity: Citing Evidence

Directions: Cite evidence from the reading selection to support each statement.

Statement

Evidence

1. Lincoln solved the problem of supplying Union troops.

Statement

Evidence

2. Grant's critics objected to him being appointed general in chief.

Statement

Evidence

3. General Sherman's attitude toward civilians changed during the course of the war.

From the Wilderness to Cold Harbor

Ulysses Grant was a survivor. He was forced to resign from the army in 1854. He reentered the army in 1861 only through political pull, and even with his record of victories, he had twice been relieved of command. In spite of Grant's critics, President Lincoln admired him as a fighter who did his best with whatever he had. After lifting the siege at Chattanooga, Grant was called to Washington, D.C., where Lincoln promoted him to lieutenant general in the Regular Army and gave him the responsibility of designing all Union strategy. Grant was an active man who preferred a saddle to a desk. He would go with the Army of the Potomac as it moved against Lee. He promised Lincoln that no matter what happened, he would not turn back.

Union artillery crossing the Rapidan River on pontoon bridges

Battle of the Wilderness

On May 4, 1864, General Grant and his army crossed the Rapidan River and moved into the region of Virginia known as the Wilderness. Although Grant planned to destroy Lee here, there was no clear winner in the three day (May 5–7) Wilderness Battle. The location suited General Lee and the Confederate Army better than Grant. The dense woods of the wilderness cancelled the Union's advantage in cavalry and artillery. Each army had its opportunity to win a major victory. General Winfield Hancock's troops broke the Confederate Army's line on May 6, but just as they came to the clearing where Lee's headquarters was, General Longstreet's fresh Confederate troops arrived and drove them back. Later that same day, Longstreet broke the Union's flank, but was shot by one of his own men as he rode back from the line. Brush fires broke out, and at times the battle stopped so the wounded could be rescued.

Battle at Spotsylvania

On May 7, the armies rested and waited for orders. That evening, the word came from Grant: the Union Army was heading south to Spotsylvania. This move was no surprise to Lee, who reasoned that if he were Grant, that would be his target. General Richard Anderson (now commanding Longstreet's men) had dug five miles of trenches before the Yankees arrived. Shaped like the letter U, the trenches allowed Confederate troops to easily move from one position to another and meet Union advances head on. Colonel Emory Upton's soldiers broke through the Confederate line, but were driven back. Then Hancock got through; Lee was there at the front to lead his soldiers, but his soldiers shouted "Go back, General Lee! Do go back! General Lee to the rear—General Lee to the rear!" His men refused to go forward until their beloved general was protected. When Lee moved off to talk with Longstreet, his men advanced and drove Hancock's men back. The weakest spot in the U became known as the "Bloody Angle" because of the fierce fighting there. The dead lay three deep in the muddy trenches at the Bloody Angle. There was no clear winner in the Battle of Spotsylvania and both sides sustained heavy causalities. Grant moved toward Cold Harbor near the Confederate capital of Richmond, Virginia.

Battle at Cold Harbor

On May 31, 1864, Union General Phil Sheridan and his cavalry seized the crossroads to Cold Harbor. The Rebel infantry arrived and was soon in position and digging in. As Union soldiers prepared a frontal attack on the Confederate line, they pinned pieces of paper with their names on them to their uniforms so their families would know where they had died. The attack began on June 3 and continued to June 12. In the end, the Confederate Army would score a victory, and Cold Harbor would be Grant's last "battle in the Wilderness."

Name: _____ Date: _____

Activity: Summarizing

Directions: Complete the graphic organizer with information from the reading selection.

Battle of the Wilderness

Summary

Battle at Spotsylvania

Summary

Battle at Cold Harbor

Summary

Sherman's March to the Sea

General William T. Sherman

When General Ulysses S. Grant took command of the Union Army, he entrusted the command of his western army to General William T. Sherman. They had first teamed up in the battles at Fort Henry and Fort Donelson and had become close friends. Like Grant, Sherman had been a failure for most of his civilian life, but then the Civil War came. At first, he had many critics who pointed out his exaggeration of Southern forces in Kentucky and who claimed he was insane.

Sherman's March To the Atlantic

Grant was promoted to general-in-chief and was going east to take charge of the campaign against Robert E. Lee, commander of the Confederate Army. Grant could no longer actively lead the army in the West, so in 1864 he entrusted that job to William T. Sherman. While Grant pressed Lee's army, Sherman was to drive toward Atlanta, Georgia, and once it was taken, to march toward the Atlantic coast. Confederate General Joe Johnston intended to block him. Knowing Sherman had the advantage of numbers, Johnston's plan was to find a good position, dig in, make the enemy pay a terrible price for the trench, and when the time came, drop back to another good defensive position. With high enough casualties, the Democrats would win the 1864 election and make peace. His army was ragged and hungry, but they were very loyal to him. Slowly withdrawing, Johnston gave up at the battles of Dalton, Resaca, Adairsville, and Kennesaw Mountain. Grant and Sherman respected his ability, but Confederate President Davis did not like him or his strategy. After his Generals Braxton Bragg and John Hood falsely accused Johnston of having no plans for the defense of Atlanta, Davis relieved Johnston of command on July 17, 1864, and appointed General John Bell Hood as his replacement.

Hood was described by Lee as "all lion and no fox." His courage was unquestioned. His arm was crippled at Gettysburg, a leg was amputated after Chickamauga, and he had to be strapped in his saddle to ride. The army was furious at the change of command, and even Hood became uncertain that he was the right choice. By this time, the Confederates were backed up to the 12 miles of trenches protecting Atlanta. Rather than wait for Sherman and his Union troops to attack, Hood sent armies out to strike them first, but the Rebels were repulsed at Peachtree Creek. General William Hardee then tried to break the Union line east of the city, but that move also failed. Sherman, however, was also having trouble. General Stephen D. Lee held off a Union advance at Ezra's Church, west of Atlanta, and General Joe Wheeler's cavalry defeated three larger Union cavalry units.

Sherman believed in "total warfare": fighting armies and destroying cities, towns, and farms along the way. He began shelling Atlanta while sending his troops in a wide arc to cut off its railroad connections to the south. Failing to drive off Union troops at Jonesboro, Hood set fire to everything of military value and left Atlanta on September 1, 1864. On September 3, Sherman sent a telegram to officials in

> **Did You Know?**
>
> Sherman estimated that his troops did 100 million dollars of damage to the South on his march to the Atlantic.

Washington that "Atlanta is ours, and fairly won." Sherman ordered everyone to leave the city, then in November, he burned the city, and his army began its famous "March to the Sea." Hood moved northward, but General George Thomas, with 60,000 Union soldiers, kept him from doing much harm. For Sherman's 62,000 men, the March to the Sea was almost a peaceful stroll. On December 21, 1864, Savannah, Georgia, fell to the Union.

Name: _____ Date: _____

Activity: Recalling Information

Directions: Answer the questions using information from the reading selection.

1. Why did critics oppose Sherman as commander of the Union's western army?

Answer:

2. What made it possible for Sherman to assume command of Union troops in the West?

Answer:

3. Who was the first Confederate commander to oppose Sherman on his march to Atlanta?

Answer:

4. How did Sherman's actions in Atlanta, Georgia, demonstrate his attitude toward war?

Answer:

The Lincoln Cabinet: Internal Civil War

If you had asked the average Republican in early 1860 who was the most important member of the party, the answer you would have most likely heard was William Seward or Salmon Chase, not Abraham Lincoln. Only six years old, the Republican Party had brought together an odd collection of members: Whigs, unhappy Democrats, members of the Free Soil Party, and reformers interested in many different causes. No one person could claim that he invented the Republican Party. Many leaders were old rivals and political enemies.

Abraham Lincoln, of the newly formed Republican Party, became the 16th president on March 6, 1861. He quickly set about choosing his Cabinet to advise him on affairs of the nation. President Lincoln purposefully appointed three of his political rivals to his Cabinet.

A Team of Rivals

William Seward took the secretary of state job because he thought it would make him the real power in government. A former governor and senator, he often made statements that caused problems for him later. Strongly anti-slavery, he said in 1850 there was a "higher law than the Constitution" and talked about an "irrepressible conflict" in an 1858 speech. He made Lincoln wonder about his new secretary of state when he suggested the U.S. make war on France and Spain and "wrap the world in flames." After a mild rebuke by Lincoln, Seward quieted down and did an effective job.

The secretary of the treasury was Salmon Chase. Like Seward, he thought he should have been the Republican presidential candidate and made no secret of his opinion that he was smarter than Lincoln. Self-righteous and without humor, he and Lincoln were much different in approach to issues and people.

Edwin Stanton became secretary of war in 1862. Stanton was a Democrat, had backed Breckinridge in 1860, and had criticized Lincoln. Yet, Lincoln chose him for his Cabinet. Stanton was very efficient and soon had the War Department operating smoothly. He was not easy to like, however.

Washington is a city that thrives on rumors, and during the Civil War, there were more than usual. A common rumor was that Lincoln was under Seward's thumb, that Seward was the "evil genius" in the administration. Lincoln and Seward knew better, but Chase believed it and talked with his Radical Republican friends (a splinter group of the Republican Party) about it. After the disaster at Fredericksburg, criticism of Lincoln was common, and rumors spread that the Cabinet—and maybe even Lincoln—were going to resign.

Seward turned in his resignation, in order to relieve pressure on Lincoln, but no one else knew that. A group of senators came to see Lincoln and blamed Seward for being lukewarm in the conduct of the war. The president said little but invited the senators to return the next day. When they came, they found all the Cabinet except Seward present, and Lincoln told them the Cabinet was always consulted, but he made all the decisions. Then Lincoln asked the Cabinet to confirm what he had said. Chase made a brief statement agreeing with the president. The next day, Chase offered to resign. Lincoln then turned down both resignations, and the Cabinet was not changed. One thing had been accomplished: Chase and Seward had both learned a valuable lesson in politics from Lincoln.

Name: _____ Date: _____

Activity: Key Details

Directions: Complete the graphic organizer using information from the reading selection.

The First Reading of the Emancipation Proclamation Before the Cabinet, *painted at the White House in 1864 by Francis B. Carpenter, engraved by A.H. Ritchie. (Left to Right: Edwin M. Stanton, Secretary of War; Salmon P. Chase, Secretary of the Treasury; President Lincoln; Gideon Welles, Secretary of the Navy; Caleb B Smith, Secretary of the Interior; William H. Seward, Secretary of State; Montgomery Blair, Postmaster General; and Edward Bates, Attorney General)*

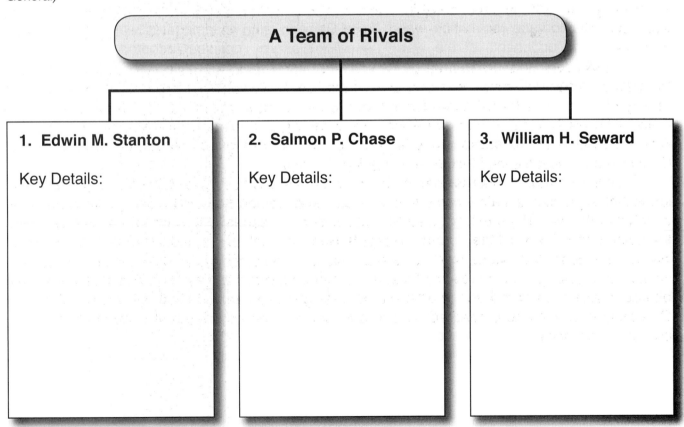

A Team of Rivals

1. Edwin M. Stanton
Key Details:

2. Salmon P. Chase
Key Details:

3. William H. Seward
Key Details:

The Election of 1864: Lincoln vs. McClellan

The U.S. Constitution requires that a presidential election be held every four years, but in most countries, a civil war might justify calling off a scheduled election. However, no one in either party suggested that the election be delayed.

Lincoln was far from confident as the Republican convention approached in 1864. Too many battles had been lost: Bull Run, Fredericksburg, and Chancellorsville among them. Victories had been hard won at Antietam, Vicksburg, and Gettysburg. Brighter days might be ahead, but would voters forget disasters of the past?

Lincoln's Critics

Critics seemed almost everywhere. Senator Ben Wade bluntly told Lincoln: "You are the father of every military blunder that has been made during the war." Others preferred to criticize him behind his back. Senator Samuel Pomeroy of Kansas issued the Pomeroy Circular, which was to be a "strictly private" letter urging that Lincoln be dropped from the ticket and Chase nominated to replace him. Chase was embarrassed and offered to resign, but Lincoln refused. Another group wanted General John C. Fremont, but so many Democrats were in that movement that no important Republican supported Fremont.

Meeting in Baltimore, the Republicans (who now called themselves the National Union Party) chose Lincoln for a second term, with Democrat Andrew Johnson for vice president. Lincoln said that the party had decided it was best not to "swap horses while crossing the river." Horace Greeley was among those who believed the party was doomed with Lincoln as the candidate, and he and others supported Fremont's Radical Democracy ticket. Fremont's group folded later and supported Lincoln.

Democratic Presidential Convention

The Democratic convention was held in Chicago, and its delegates were split between supporters and opponents of the war. The party platform (policies) adopted called for both continuing the war and for peace. The candidate chosen was George B. McClellan, the twice-removed general. McClellan tried to separate himself from the Peace Democrats, but Republicans would not let the Democratic platform die as an issue.

Military Support for Lincoln

Lincoln needed help to win, and his generals cooperated. General Sheridan's campaign in the Shenandoah Valley was so successful that James Garfield called it "a speech ... more powerful and valuable to the Union cause than all the stumpers in the Republic." General Custer displayed captured enemy battle flags in Washington. But even more useful were the 10,000 soldiers sent home by Sheridan to vote in the presidential election. Of soldiers who cast absentee votes, three out of four voted for Lincoln.

Election Results

In electoral votes, Lincoln won 212 to 12. McClellan carried only three states. In the House, Republicans outnumbered Democrats 145 to 40, and in the Senate, the margin was 41 to 10. Even though Lincoln would deliver his second inaugural message on March 4, 1865, the war continued to be fought.

Name: _____ Date: _____

Activity: Compare and Contrast

Directions: Complete the graphic organizer using information from the reading selection.

President Abraham Lincoln	President Abraham Lincoln and General George B. McClellan were both presidential candidates in the election of 1864.	General George B. McClellan

Political Party		**Political Party**
Problems for the Candidate		**Problems for the Candidate**
Election Outcome		**Election Outcome**

The South During the War

The four years of war discouraged all but the most devoted Confederates. Faced with enormous prices for everything, a shopper went into the store with a wheelbarrow full of cash to buy a sack full of groceries. The soldier wondered if he should not desert and care for his starving family. Those who were in battle areas or were driven out of their homes by Yankee soldiers became refugees, looking for a meal to eat and a place to lie down at night. The transportation system was being destroyed by Sherman's troops. Gangs of hoodlums, including deserters of both armies, picked on the helpless and, in some areas, simply took over.

A Confederate bond used as money by the Confederate government during the Civil War

Problems for the South

There were shortages of almost everything. Food was in short supply, especially in cities where speculators held out for higher prices. This led to rioting and looting in Richmond, Virginia, the Confederate capital. In April 1862, a mob attacked warehouses and smashed store windows grabbing jewelry and shoes. President Davis arrived and appealed to the mob to go home. He threw them some money and, to show it was all he had, he turned his pockets inside out. Then he pulled out his watch and told them that if they were not gone in five minutes, he would order the militia to fire on them. The crowd disappeared, but the food shortage only got worse.

Crime rose as law and order collapsed. By 1864, in some parts of the South, there were no sheriffs or police to arrest the criminals and no judges to hear their cases. Deserters gathered in the mountains, swamps, and remote areas and literally took over. In a few cases, the Confederate Army was sent to round them up, but this took troops away from the war and did not solve the problem.

Money was at the root of both food and crime problems. Secretary of Treasury Christopher Memminger urged the Confederate Congress to pay for the war with taxes, but he was ignored. The Confederacy assumed that citizen loyalty would be weakened by heavy taxes. At first they were able to get around the money shortage by seizing federal assets. Then they tried borrowing. In 1862, Erlanger & Co. in Paris agreed to market Confederate bonds in return for a large commission for itself. At first the bonds sold well, but sales dropped quickly after the battles of Gettysburg and Vicksburg. All else failing, the Confederacy printed money at a rapid pace.

Refugees were chased from their homes either as the result of battles in their backyards or because General Sherman or some other Union officer ordered them out. It is estimated that about 175,000 to 200,000 Southerners were refugees for an extended period of time. Usually they drifted to cities or tried to find a family member who would take them in. Those most accepted were ministers, teachers, and physicians. The least wanted were proud aristocrats, the poor, and draft dodgers.

The South's enthusiasm for war was declining after the summer of 1863, and only grim determination to hold on was left in its place.

Name: _____ Date: _____

Activity: Cause and Effect

Directions: Complete the graphic organizer using information from the reading selection.

Cause #1

Food was in short supply, especially in cities where speculators held out for higher prices.

Effect

Cause #2

There was a shortage of money.

Effect

Cause #3

Crime rose as law and order collapsed.

Effect

Cause #4

Sherman and other Union generals chased Southerners from their homes.

Effect

Petersburg Is Besieged

The Confederate Army was being taken apart, one big chunk after another. When Vicksburg fell in 1863, the western part of the Confederacy was sliced off from the east. Then General Sherman's march of Union troops to Atlanta was beginning to carve off Mississippi, Alabama, Florida, and southern Georgia. The Union Army could draft more men and build more guns, but the South was about out of able-bodied men, and its food and military resources were running low. The South was almost taking pride in its stubborn refusal to quit. If President Lincoln were to lose the 1864 election, the Confederacy might yet be able to make peace with a more reasonable George McClellan administration, a twice-removed general from the Lincoln administration.

Fort Sedgwick, a Union fort in the siege line around Petersburg, blocked one of the main roads in and out of the town.

Both Armies Create Diversions

To describe what happened during this time in an orderly way is almost impossible. General Ulysses S. Grant and General Robert E. Lee were both trying to create diversions, pulling the enemy away from the main army. During the Wilderness campaign, Grant had sent General Ben Butler with 33,000 men to attack Petersburg, Virginia. Confederate General P.G.T. Beauregard, with 2,000 men, put up enough resistance at the town of Bermuda Hundred, outside of Richmond, Virginia, that Butler dug in. On May 16, 1864, when Butler tried to capture the Fort at Drewry's Bluff, the South's 20,000 men pushed the Yankees back with heavy losses.

In June, the main body of Grant's troops, a 100,000-man army, began to move southward. For a few days, Lee had no idea where Grant was and barely arrived with the main part of his army in time to block Grant's capture of Petersburg on June 15. Like lions they faced each other, one too hungry to attack and the other too tired and hot to renew the battle.

General Philip Sheridan was sent north and west to pull Lee's Confederate cavalry away and destroy railroads leading to Richmond. Confederate cavalry units, led by Generals Wade Hampton and Fitzhugh Lee, were able to force back Sherman's Union troops at the battle of Trevilian Station in Virginia on June 11, 1864, but not until Sherman had temporarily damaged a railroad.

In July, Confederate General Jubal Early was sent north with 8,000 ragged men to pressure President Lincoln to recall all or part of Grant's army to Washington, D.C. Meeting no opposition at first, the Confederates moved into Maryland and came close enough to Washington's defenses to see the Capitol dome. On July 12, 1864, Confederate troops attacked Fort Stevens but were pushed back by Union troops. President Lincoln watched the battle from the fort. General Early withdrew and went on to Pennsylvania, where his troops burned Chambersburg. On September 21, 1864, Early returned to Virginia, where General Sheridan's troops defeated him at Winchester at the Battle of Fisher's Hill, but his men returned the favor later at the Battle of Cedar Creek on October 19, 1864.

On July 30, 1864, at the Battle of the Crater in Petersburg, Virginia, an unusual method of relieving the siege was tried; some Pennsylvania coal miners suggested digging a tunnel to the Confederate line and exploding a mine. General Ambrose E Burnside supported the plan, but General George Meade and General Grant were less than enthused about its chances of working. During the battle, an explosion destroyed 170 feet of the line, creating a hole 30 feet deep. Union soldiers went into the crater rather than around it, making them easy targets. Over 4,000 Union soldiers were killed. Grant called it "a stupendous failure," and Lincoln relieved Burnside of his command.

Name: _____ Date: _____

Activity: Timeline

Directions: Complete the graphic organizer using information from the reading selection. Fill in the event for each date on the timeline.

Events of 1864

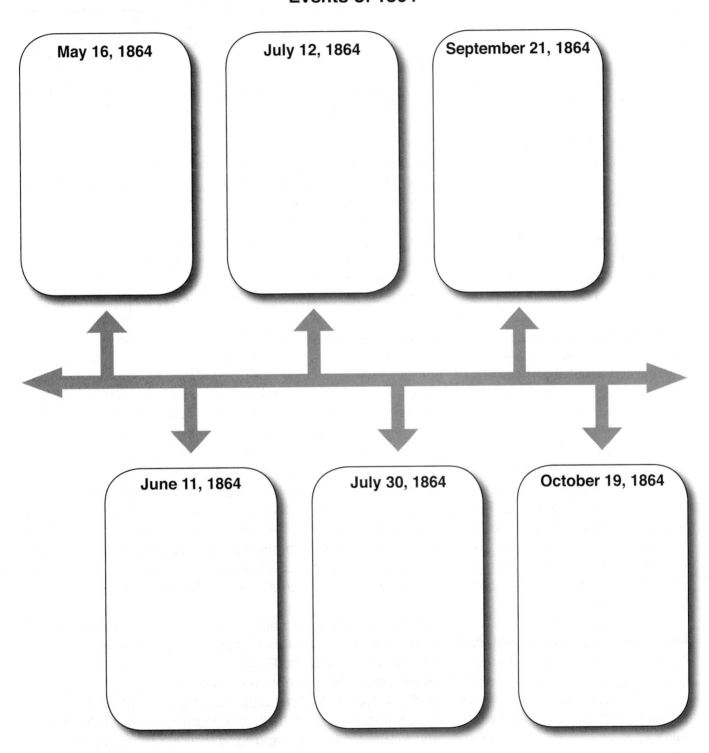

May 16, 1864

July 12, 1864

September 21, 1864

June 11, 1864

July 30, 1864

October 19, 1864

The Meeting at Appomattox

It was April once again, nearly four years since Fort Sumter; this was the time to plant the year's crops. For the farmers who made up the bulk of the Confederate Army, thoughts were drifting away to home. Some could not resist the temptation to desert; they knew that Grant's army was getting larger, and his supplies were increasing daily. They also knew there was no food for them, and even if they were paid, the money was worthless. Why not go back to take care of family needs? Others were determined to see it through to the end; they had put too much of their lives into this cause to quit before it was over.

Wilmer McLean's house in Appomattox, Virginia, where General Grant and General Lee met to discuss the terms of surrender

Events Leading Up to the End of the War

To the south, General Sherman was meeting organized resistance again. After Lee was appointed general-in-chief, he had reappointed Joe Johnston in February 1865 to command an army of 22,000 men against Sherman, who now had 90,000 men. As in the past, Johnston's tactic was to give ground, but punch whenever a good opportunity presented itself.

General Grant's Union troops kept extending their line around Petersburg, Virginia, and Lee realized that unless he did something soon, his army would be stretched so thin that he would easily be defeated by a sudden Yankee thrust anywhere along the line. Some engagements in the last weeks of the siege at Petersburg were as fierce as any in the war. On March 25, 1865, the Rebels captured Fort Stedman, a major earthwork on the Union line. The thrill of victory was brief, and the next day, most of the Confederates involved were dead, injured, or captured.

The next major engagement was at Five Forks, where General Sheridan's cavalry clashed with Rebels on March 30 and April 1. After suffering heavy casualties there, Lee, realizing he could no longer hold Petersburg, sent a message to President Davis that he was withdrawing. He then planned his next move. He would head west to Amelia Courthouse on the Richmond & Danville Railroad. Once there, his men would head south to join with Johnston and the Confederate Army of Tennessee. The withdrawal did not fool Grant, and Union troops were in hot pursuit, capturing stragglers and supply trains.

Surrender at Appomattox Courthouse

On April 9, Lee knew he was cut off and could not make it to Amelia Courthouse. A time was arranged to meet with Grant and discuss terms of surrender. Wilmer McLean's house in Appomattox Courthouse, Virginia, was selected as the meeting place.

Some of Lee's officers wanted to form guerilla units and live off the land, but Lee opposed that idea, and they gave in to his wishes. Much has been written about the meeting. Lee wore a dress uniform, Grant, coming off the battlefield, a dirty coat and mud-covered boots. After small talk about their service together in the Mexican War, Lee asked Grant for the terms of surrender and found them to be generous. The Confederate troops would be paroled, given rations, and allowed to take their horses and mules home with them.

As the news spread, there was great joy among the Union soldiers. Then the ragged but proud Army of Northern Virginia stacked their arms, and there was silence as soldiers who had fought so hard now faced each other in peace. For all present, the moment would never be forgotten.

Name: _____ Date: _____

Activity: Summarizing

Directions: Complete the graphic organizer using information from the reading selection.

Surrender at Appomattox

Ulysses S. Grant

1. Which army did General Grant command during the Civil War?

   Answer: _____

Robert E. Lee

2. Which army did General Lee command during the Civil War?

   Answer: _____

3. Summarize the surrender at Appomattox.

The Confederate Government Collapses

The ruins of Richmond, Virginia

On April 2, 1865, there was a rush of activity as government officials in Richmond scurried around closing up their offices, then raced home to pack their bags and arrange for transportation out of town. The end of the war was different from what they had envisioned at the beginning. In 1861, the South thought the North would let them secede without a fight. They believed that if a war did occur one Rebel could whip ten Yankees. Later, they pinned their hopes on the superior generalship of Lee and Jackson. They thought the costal blockade could be broken with ironclads ripping holes in wooden Union ships. They hoped England would come to help because their textile mills would be starved for Confederate cotton. But in the end, what they hoped for and believed in did not happen.

Mistakes Made by the Confederate Government

It is easier to spot the mistakes of the past than it is to prevent them from happening in our own time. The following mistakes made by the Confederate government are not listed in order of importance, but in the approximate order that they occurred.

- The Confederacy had underestimated Lincoln. He was a country lawyer with little national experience. He was not much of a public speaker, yet people understood him. He seemed slow to make decisions, but once they were made, he usually picked the best way to go.
- In the early days of the blockade, it was very easy to get supplies through. It would have been an ideal time to bring in far more arms, gunpowder, medicine, and other vital items than the Confederacy actually did. After losing Port Royal, Norfolk, New Orleans, and Mobile Bay, the South was running short on good ports through which supplies could be delivered.
- "King Cotton diplomacy" assumed that if England and France were cut off from Southern cotton, they would be forced to recognize the independence of the South. This did not happen. Instead, the greatest effect of the "diplomacy" was to hurt the South's ability to buy supplies and arms.
- The decision not to tax put a burden on the public far worse than any reasonable tax could. The lack of a tax meant the government had no revenue source to support war efforts. Instead, they printed their own money and expected their citizens to provide food and supplies. When money became worthless and people were forced to barter, their opinion of the government must have suffered.
- Slaves were counted on to help win the war, and during the war there were no massive slave rebellions, but work slowed down to a near stop on many farms. General Patrick Cleburne had requested slaves be allowed to fight for the Confederacy, but it wasn't until March 18, 1865, that legislation was passed making it legal for black soldiers to serve. This measure was a little too late, as black soldiers had been fighting for the Union Army since early in 1863.

Activity: Research

Go online to <https://www.youtube.com/watch?v=J5YJsiRCZHw> to watch an overview of the American Civil War.

Name: _____ Date: _____

Activity: Recalling Information

Directions: Complete the graphic organizer using information from the reading selection.

Mistakes Made by the Confederate Government

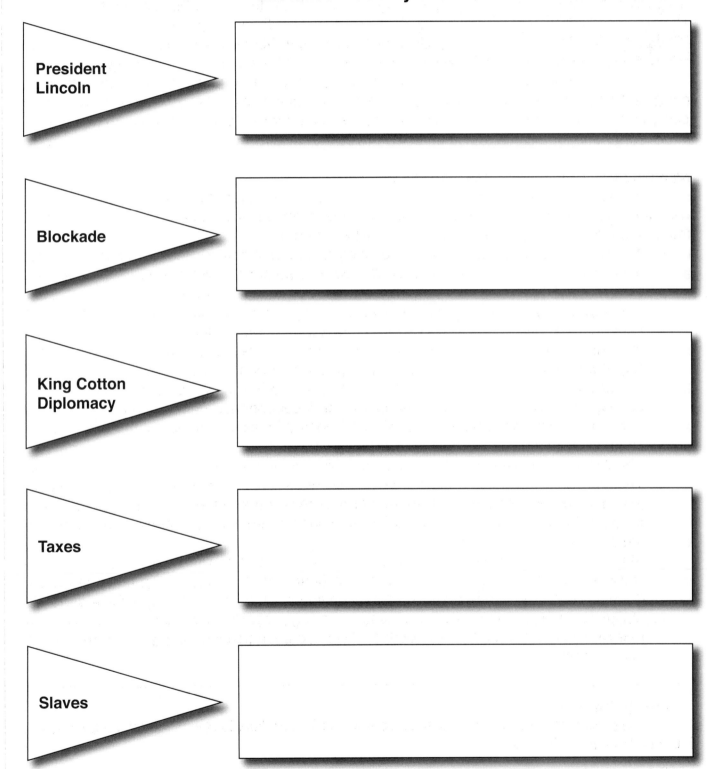

President Lincoln

Blockade

King Cotton Diplomacy

Taxes

Slaves

Lincoln Is Assassinated

Many Southerners blamed Lincoln for the Civil War. An actor, John Wilkes Booth, more famous for dramatic actions on the stage than for the way he delivered lines, was one of them. A Confederate sympathizer, he wanted to do something dramatic to turn the war around. His original plan was to capture Lincoln and use him as a hostage until Confederate prisoners of war were released. He brought several men into his plot, but by April 1865, some had lost interest in the scheme.

John Wilkes Booth

Booth Desperate to Help the South

The news of the fall of Richmond, the Confederate capital, and General Robert E. Lee's surrender on April 9 to General Ulysses S. Grant at Appomattox Courthouse hit Booth hard. He decided a different plan to help the South would have to be found. The idea came to him of killing President Lincoln, Vice President Andrew Johnson, and Secretary of State Seward. His hope was to throw the Union government into chaos, and perhaps the Confederacy could then reorganize resistance. When Booth checked his mail at Ford's Theater on April 14, he was told that Lincoln would attend the evening's performance of *Our American Cousin.* Booth called his little band of followers together and handed out assignments. George Atzerodt was to kill Johnson, and Lewis Powell was to kill Seward. Booth reserved the honor of assassinating Lincoln for himself. After a few drinks at a saloon, Booth went to the theater and made his final preparations for his most dramatic performance.

Lincoln Assassinated at Ford's Theater

President and Mrs. Lincoln had planned on taking General and Mrs. Grant with them to the play, but the Grants were not going to be in town. Instead, they took Major Henry Rathbone and his fiancée, Clara Harris. The bodyguard for the evening was John Parker, who left his seat outside the presidential box to find a seat where he could watch the play.

Booth entered the theater after the play had begun, found the president's box unguarded, and came up behind Lincoln with a Derringer in one hand and a knife in the other. He shot the president at pointblank range and prepared to leap from the box. Rathbone grabbed his arm, and Booth slashed him with the knife. Then Booth jumped, but as he fell, he caught his spur in the bunting draped from the box. He landed off-balance and broke his leg. As he staggered across the stage, he shouted, "Sic simper tyrannis" (meaning "Thus always to tyrants"). Then he hobbled out the stage door and rode off. President Lincoln was carefully carried across the street to a nearby boardinghouse. Lincoln never regained consciousness and died the following morning.

Booth escaped to Maryland with a fellow conspirator. On April 26, Booth was surrounded in a barn near Port Royal, Virginia. He was shot and died a few hours later. The other assassins failed in their tasks. Atzerodt never made any effort to kill Johnson, and Powell's efforts to kill Seward by stabbing him failed.

Activity: Primary Source

Go online to <http://digital.library.mcgill.ca/lincoln/exhibit/imgdisplay.php?item=3&sec=4&taft=> and read the journal entries of Dr. C. S. Taft who attended President Lincoln after he was shot.

Name: _____ Date: _____

Activity: Recalling Information

Directions: Complete the graphic organizer using information from the reading selection.

Question	Answer

1. What did Booth hope to accomplish with his original scheme to capture Lincoln and hold him hostage?

2. What event caused Booth to develop a plan to assassinate President Lincoln?

3. What did Booth hope to accomplish with the assassination of President Lincoln?

4. Who were the other assassins involved in Booth's plan?

The Impact of the War

The Civil War lasted four years and was the most devastating war in American history with over 600,000 casualties. Fighting started at Fort Sumter in South Carolina on April 12, 1861. The war ended on April 9, 1865, at Wilmer McLean's house in Appomattox Courthouse, Virginia. The terms of surrender were signed by Generals Robert E. Lee and Ulysses S. Grant. The Civil War saved the Union, but changed the nation forever.

People from the North who moved to the South in order to make a profit off Reconstruction efforts were called carpetbaggers. Cartoon by Thomas Nast

Slavery

The war ended slavery. President Lincoln issued the Emancipation Proclamation on January 1, 1863. This document proclaimed that any slave held in the rebellious states "are, and henceforward shall be free." Lincoln allowed black soldiers to fight for the Union, and before his death, he supported the passage of the Thirteenth Amendment that would officially end slavery in the United States. The Thirteenth Amendment was ratified on December 6, 1865, approximately seven months after his death.

The South

The Civil War caused billions of dollars of damage to the South. Towns and cities, large plantations, small farms, roads, bridges, and railroads were left in ruins. The destruction caused by the war forced the South to begin an era of Reconstruction; a period of time filled with bribery and corruption.

The North

The Civil War changed northern industry. Small shops were replaced by large factories. Businessmen went from selling to local markets to national markets. Even in agriculture, the small farmer who tried to get by without expensive equipment was doomed to lose out to his neighbor who was equipped with the latest thresher, planter, or harvester.

Westward Expansion

The Civil War would change the course of westward expansion. In May 1862, Congress passed the Homestead Act offering free land to homesteaders to encourage settlement of western territory. After the war, many former soldiers moved to the West. Congress also passed the Pacific Railroad Act in 1862. This law chartered two railroad companies, the Central Pacific and the Union Pacific, with the job of building a transcontinental railroad that would link the United States from east to west. In 1869, the Central Pacific and Union Pacific Railroads met at Promontory Point, Utah, making transportation of people and goods from the Atlantic to the Pacific faster and easier.

Name: _____ Date: _____

Activity: Event and Impact

Directions: Complete the graphic organizer using information from the reading selection.

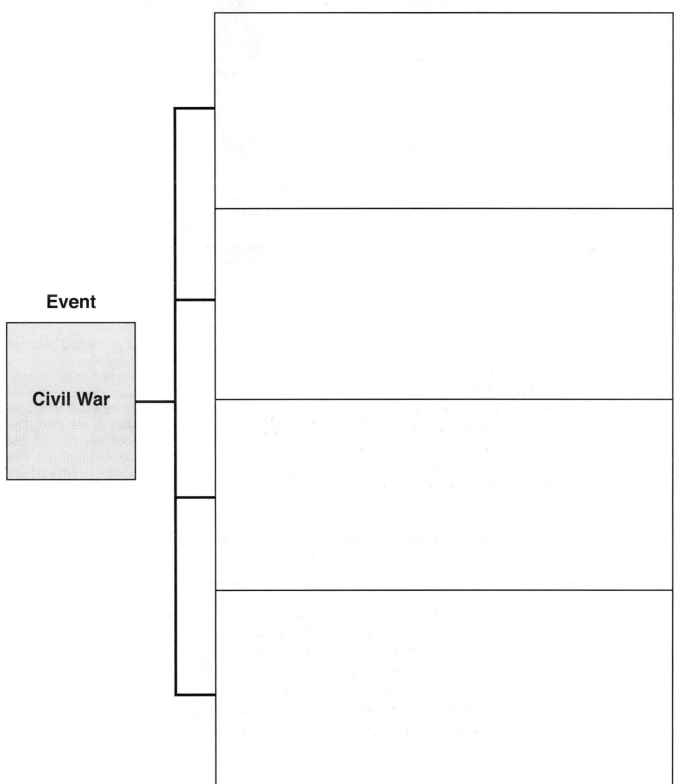

Impact

Event

Civil War

Answer Keys

Activity: Recalling Information (p. 3)

1. A doctrine that stated if Congress went too far, a state had the right to prevent a law from being enforced inside its boundaries.
2. A movement that proposed sending free African Americans to Africa or finding an isolated place for them in Central America as a solution to slavery.
3. North: excited by change; found prosperity in business and trade; used low-paid immigrants to do the hardest jobs in factories; governed by middle-class politicians
South: preferred tradition; valued land; used slave labor; gave power to aristocrats called planters

Activity: Key Details (p. 5)

(Answers will vary but may include:)

Planters: top of Southern society; owned more than 20 slaves; might own several plantations; lived in great mansions; reinvested wealth in more land, horses, and slaves

Merchants/Professionals: influential; many owned slaves; wanted to become planters; largest customers were the planters; farmers had fewer than 20 slaves

Poor Whites: bottom of white society; often illiterate and isolated; looked down upon by others; ignored by rich people

Free Blacks: less than 10% of blacks in the South were free; lived in cities where it was easier to find work

Slaves: bottom of Southern society; used for labor-intensive agricultural work; hired out to other planters or tradesmen

Activity: Summarizing (p. 7)

(Answers will vary but may include:)

Technology: The reaper, steel plow, and other inventions brought technological changes to agriculture. These changes caused farmers to migrate to states like Illinois, Indiana, and Michigan, causing the population of these states to explode. Production of food increased, and it was possible to begin exporting some of it to Europe. In the Northeast, textile mills flourished using southern cotton and northern wool. People invested in new technologies, such as sewing machines, revolvers, and pneumatic tires, causing an increase in employment in manufacturing.

Transportation: Railroads were taking customers away from turnpikes, stagecoach lines, freighters, and steamboats. Between 1850 and 1860 the number of miles of track more than tripled. The North had more miles of track than the South, and their railroads were "better equipped and maintained."

Communication Networks: By 1860, there were 50,000 miles of telegraph line. A Trans-Atlantic cable was laid in 1858.

Attitudes: People who lived in the North were more inclined toward reform movements: temperance, women's suffrage, and anti-slavery. An individual might belong to multiple reform movements. Northerners were interested in acquiring financial success, while acquiring more slaves and landholdings were important to Southerners. Northerners felt that Southerners were too preoccupied with slavery and needed to change their way of thinking.

Activity: Event and Effect (p. 9)

Event 1: raised the issue of whether states should be admitted as free or slave states; Southerners threaten secession

Event 2: allowed California to be admitted as a free state, New Mexico and Utah Territories to be organized with no reference to slavery, a stronger fugitive slave law would be passed, and slave trading would end in the District of Columbia

Event 3: brought new converts to the abolitionist movement; caused Northerners to question how much they should concede to the South

Event 4: split Democrats, destroyed the Whigs, and created the Republican Party; Charles Sumner assaulted; murders and raids in Kansas

Activity: Summarizing (p. 11)

Main Idea: The case of *Dred Scott v. Sanford* declared the Missouri Compromise unconstitutional.
Summary: Dred Scott was a slave taken by his master into territory declared free by the Missouri Compromise. His master died. Since Scott was residing in a free territory, people questioned if he was a free man. The Missouri Supreme Court decided Scott was not free, but the case was appealed to the U.S. Supreme Court. The U.S. Supreme Court decided that Scott was not a citizen of either Missouri or the United States, and the Missouri Compromise was unconstitutional because territories existed "for the common use and equal benefit of all." Southerners rejoiced over the decision, but it angered Northerners.
Main Idea: Abraham Lincoln's candidacy in the election of 1858 made him famous.
Summary: The Illinois U.S. senatorial election of 1858 was between incumbent Stephen Douglas and his opponent Abraham Lincoln. At that time, state legislatures elected senators. Douglas was well-dressed and gifted in public speaking. Abraham Lincoln, an attorney, was tall, had a rugged appearance, and used clever sayings when he spoke. The two participated in a series of debates. Lincoln lost the election to Douglas, but his fame for debating helped him when he decided to run for president in 1860.
Main Idea: John Brown was an abolitionist who led the raid on Harpers Ferry.

Summary: John Brown was a strong abolitionist. He raided a pro-slavery community in Kansas. Five men and boys were killed. He stole 11 slaves from Missouri and took them to Canada. Then he planned an attack to free all slaves. His plan was to capture the federal arsenal at Harpers Ferry, Virginia. He would begin a great revolt by arming slaves in the area. He captured the arsenal, but was later arrested for the crime. He was found guilty and hanged. Some Northerners thought he was a hero, but others did not.

Activity: Recalling Information (p. 13)
(Answers will vary but may include:)
1. John Bell—Constitutional Union Party; Abraham Lincoln—Republican Party; Stephen Douglas—Democratic Party (Northern); John Breckinridge—Democratic Party (Southern)
2. the right of states to control slavery, a railroad to the Pacific, a homestead act, and a protective tariff
3. When the Democrats met at their convention in Charleston, they were unable to agree on a candidate. They met again in Baltimore, but Southern delegates walked out. Northern delegates chose a candidate. Southerners met again and chose their own candidate.
4. President Buchanan opposed secession, but he did not know what to do. He believed he did not have the right to force states to stay in the Union.

Activity: Sequence of Events (p. 15)
April 10, 1861: Fort Sumter ordered to surrender
April 12, 1861: Firing on Fort Sumter begins
April 14, 1861: Anderson surrenders Fort Sumter
April 15, 1861: Lincoln calls for 75,000 volunteers
April 17, 1861: Virginia secedes from Union
May 6, 1861: Arkansas secedes from Union
May 20, 1861: North Carolina secedes from Union

Activity: Compare and Contrast (p. 17)
(Answers will vary but may include:)
Alike: served in military; initially opposed secession; served in Congress; criticized by the press; accused of acting like dictators; had a Congress who had other priorities than winning the war; did not let the heads of departments do their jobs; showed personal courage in dangerous situations; accused of not doing everything possible to end the war
Education
Lincoln: no formal education; studied to be a lawyer
Davis: attended university and West Point
Military Experience
Lincoln: militia captain during the Black Hawk War of 1832; little to no battle experience
Davis: West Point trained, fought in the Mexican War; wounded in battle

Political Life
Lincoln: skilled politician; served four terms in the Illinois state legislature and one term in Congress
Davis: didn't enjoy politics; served terms in both the House and Senate; Secretary of War
Attitude Toward Presidency
Lincoln: sought the office of president
Davis: didn't want to be president

Activity: Making a Comparison (p. 19)
(Answers will vary but may include:)
Territorial Departments
Union: armies were named after the major river flowing near where they operated
Confederate: armies were named after the state or the region in which they operated
Company
Union: companies had 83 to 101 officers and men
Confederate: companies more loosely organized; officers included 1 captain, 2 lieutenants, 5 sergeants, 8 corporals, and a teamster
Regiments
Union: infantry and cavalry regiments; commanded by a colonel; officers were a lieutenant colonel, major, adjutant, quartermaster, 3 surgeons, and a chaplain; regiments numbered in the order formed
Confederate: organized the same as the Union
Brigades, Divisions, Corps
Union: brigades were numbered; corps commanded by major generals
Confederate: brigades were named after commanding officer; corps commanded by lieutenant generals

Activity: Recalling Information (p. 21)
1. infantry
2. The end of the charge was the most critical, because the charge ended with hand-to-hand combat.
3. Artillery broke up charges and was used during sieges. Also, it was used to soften up the enemy in preparation of a charge.
4. 1,500–2,500 yards
5. The cavalry was used to scout enemy positions.
6. The cavalry could be used to quickly plug holes in a line. The cavalrymen would dismount and fight like infantry soldiers.

Activity: Supporting Details (p. 23)
1. All of Johnston's field commanders were either West Point graduates or Mexican War veterans. McDowell's officers were not as well trained and experienced.
2. The author called the spectators "picnickers." This indicates the spectators saw the battle as a form of entertainment. Also, most people believed that the war would be short, with one major battle deciding the outcome. The spectators probably wanted to be able to tell others that they had witnessed the battle that decided the outcome of the conflict.

3. At first, McDowell's attack was succeeding. When three retreating Confederate brigades climbed Henry House Hill, they found Confederate General Thomas Jackson waiting with a full brigade in battle formation. The retreating Confederate brigades formed up with Jackson's brigade and forced McDowell's Union Army to retreat, which led to a Confederate victory.

Activity: Key Details (p. 25)
(Answers will vary but may include:)

Government: wrote a constitution similar to the U.S. Constitution; chose Jefferson Davis as provisional president; Richmond selected as capital

Uniforms: militia units dressed in almost every style of uniform; official color was cadet gray, but not enough dye to have all units dressed the same; many soldiers dressed in butternut-colored uniforms; men used whatever they came with or could afford; generals didn't usually wear fancy uniforms; shortage of winter coats, shoes, or boots; cavalry wore yellow stripes on their pants, artillery wore red, and infantry wore blue

Flag: "Stars and Bars" first official flag; battle flag adopted in September 1861 (flag most commonly associated with the Confederacy); 1863, the "Stainless Banner," adopted to prevent confusion; "Last National" flag adopted in March 1865

Economy: borrowed money instead of taxing citizens; printed money without any gold or silver to back it up; stopped selling cotton to Europe to force England and France to recognize Confederate independence; no money to buy supplies and arms

Activity: Recalling Information (p. 27)
Union Blockades Coastline

Who?: Abraham Lincoln, Gideon Welles, Gustavus Fox

What?: ordered a blockade; stop cotton from leaving the South and arms and supplies from coming into Southern ports

When?: five days after Fort Sumter fell

Where?: coastline from South Carolina to Texas (later added coastlines of Virginia and North Carolina)

Why?: to keep the Confederacy from getting arms and supplies and to prevent them from shipping products to foreign ports

The Confederate Response

Who?: Stephen Mallory

What?: given task to find ways to break the blockade

Why?: to open ports for receiving arms and supplies and to ship out Southern products to foreign ports

How?: turned a sunken steamer into an ironclad; tried building submarines; commerce raiders attacked Northern shipping, forcing Union ships to pull out of the blockade and giving chase; privately owned blockade runners used to break through the blockade to deliver supplies

Activity: Analyzing a Primary Source (p. 29)
(Answers will vary but may include:)

1. Grant knew Generals Pillow and Floyd and believed they were poor leaders. In Excerpt One, Grant says he would be able to walk up to within gunshot of any entrenchment held by General Pillow, and that Floyd was "no soldier." Grant had attended West Point with Buckner. When Buckner surrendered Fort Donelson to Grant, he tells Grant that if he was in command Grant "would not have got up to Donelson as easily as" he did. Grant replied that if Buckner had been in command, he would not "have tried in the way I did." Grant's reply shows he respects Buckner's ability to lead.

2. The information in the reading selection supports Grant's view of the poor leadership of Generals Pillow and Floyd. It describes how General Pillow attempts to break through Grant's lines, but loses "his nerve" and retreats back to the fort. General Forrest, who had cleared the way for Pillow, was mad at Pillow for retreating. The acting Post Commander General John Floyd sides with Pillow. Together the two generals decide to surrender the fort, but not wanting the responsibility, they make General Simon Buckner, the third man in charge, do it. The reading selection also reveals why Buckner was the one having to surrender the fort as described in Excerpt Two.

Activity: Making Inferences (p. 31)
(Answers will vary but may include:)

1. The CSS *Virginia,* an ironclad, did make a mistake by waiting until the next morning to destroy the wooden-hulled USS *Minnesota.* The delay allowed the USS *Monitor,* an ironclad, to come to the aid of the *Minnesota.* This resulted in a four-and-a-half-hour battle. The *Virginia* had to retreat.

2. The CSS *Virginia* showed that wooden-hulled ships were helpless in battle against an ironclad. Also, the *Virginia* destroyed three Union ships during the one-day battle.

Activity: Summarizing (p. 33)
(Answers will vary but may include)

Lee: He orders General "Stonewall" Jackson to threaten the Union armies in the Shenandoah Valley. Later, he orders Stuart and his men to "discover enemy positions, and strength." He decided to risk sending most of the army north of the river to crush the V Corps.

Jackson: Jackson and his "foot cavalry," catch the Union Army by surprise one time after another. Jackson then rejoins the main Confederate force facing McClellan.

Magruder: His small army of 10,000 men built earthworks to block Union troops.

Johnston: After McClellan divides his army, Johnston, commander of the Confederate's Yorktown line, seizes the opportunity and attacks McClellan's divided army.

Stuart: Stuart rides behind McClellan's army, gathering information, tearing up a railroad, and taking prisoners. When he finishes his mission, he leads his men back around the enemy.

Activity: Skim and Scan (p. 35)
1. Lee   2. Longstreet   3. Johnston   4. Early
5. Longstreet   6. Johnston   7. Jackson
8. Jackson   9. Lee   10. Stuart

Activity: Map Skills (p. 37)
1. Teacher verification is required.
2. Teacher verification is required.
3. It would cut the Confederacy in two, and give control of the Mississippi River and its ports to the Union. Then the Confederates couldn't use the river to transport troops and supplies.

Activity: Key Details (p. 39)
Delaware: did not secede from the Union

Maryland: lawmakers passed resolutions supporting the Union

Kentucky: legislature voted to proclaim neutrality and forbade either the United States or the Confederacy to operate within its borders; the South broke the state's neutrality; the legislature invited Union troops in to drive the Rebels out; did not secede from the Union

Missouri: Governor Claiborne Jackson refused Lincoln's call for troops and tried to seize the U.S. federal arsenal at St. Louis; Lincoln appoints a provisional government, the Department of the Missouri (which included western Kentucky), to watch over affairs of the state; Missouri kept in Union hands throughout war

Activity: Research (p. 41)
Teacher verification is required.

Activity: Fact and Opinion (p. 43)
Teacher verification is required.

Activity: Problem and Solution (p. 45)
No Ambulances: Early in the war, someone had to carry a wounded man to the surgeon. Later, horse-drawn ambulances moved the wounded.

Nurses and Volunteers Needed: A civilian organization, the U.S. Sanitary Commission, supplied nurses to general hospitals. The Women's Relief Society in the South sent volunteers to bathe, bandage, and comfort the wounded.

No Organized Field Hospitals: Dressing stations to attend to the wounded were set up on the battlefield. Then the wounded were sent to a hospital located in the rear. Finally, the wounded were either discharged or sent back to their unit.

Shortage of Hospitals: New hospitals were built. Existing buildings (colleges, warehouses, hotels, and railroad depots) were converted into hospitals.

Activity: Making Inferences (p. 47)
(Answers will vary but may include:)
Rappahannock River: Burnside planned to cross the Rappahannock River at Fredericksburg and race to the Confederate capital of Richmond before Lee's army could stop him. Burnside planned to use pontoon bridges to cross the river, but the bridges were delivered two weeks late. This gave Lee time to move his army to block the crossing of Union troops.

Crescent-shaped Line of Hills: A line of hills surrounded Fredericksburg, Virginia. During the attack, Union soldiers were mowed down by Confederate artillery positioned on the hills.

Sunken Road: Union soldiers were trying to reach the sunken road in order to travel to Richmond. However, General Longstreet had placed 2,500 Confederate riflemen behind a stone wall that protected the sunken road. As Union soldiers advanced, the stone wall and the riflemen prevented them from reaching the road, and "bodies continued to pile up in front of the wall."

Activity: Cause and Effect (p. 49)
North

Effect: Military service was required of all able-bodied men between 20–45 years of age for three years.

Effect: A riot to protest the draft occurred in New York City. It lasted from July 13–17, 1863.

Effect: "Bounty brokers" were hired to find men to fill the draft quota.

South

Effect: At the beginning of the war, military service was required of men from ages 18 to 35. By 1864, it included those from 17 to 50.

Effect: A bill was passed in March 1865 that allowed slaves to fight for the Confederate States of America.

Effect: By 1863, ads appeared in newspapers offering $6,000 for an acceptable substitute for men being drafted.

Activity: Problem and Solution (p. 51)
1. Congress passed the Morrill Tariff in 1861. This was an excise tax on the sale of some luxury items. They also passed an income-tax law.
2. In May 1862, Congress passed the Homestead Act offering free land to homesteaders to encourage settlement of western territory.
3. Congress passed the Pacific Railroad Act in 1862. The law chartered two railroad companies, the Central Pacific and the Union Pacific, with the job of building a transcontinental railroad that would link the United States from east to west.

Activity: Summarizing (p. 53)
(Answers will vary, but may include:)

<u>Women Spies</u>: Women acted as spies. Rose Greenhow and Belle Boyd were both spies for the Confederate Army. Elizabeth Van Lew and her former slave, Mary Bowser, provided useful information to the Union Army. Many spies whose identities were never revealed kept leaders informed on the movement of enemy troops.

<u>Women Volunteers</u>: Many women volunteered as nurses. President Lincoln gave Dorothea Dix the title of Superintendent of U.S. Army Nurses. Clara Barton served as a battlefield nurse during the war and was given the title of Superintendent of Nurses for the Army of the James. Mary Bickerdyke did much to improve the quality of care for wounded soldiers. Dr. Mary Walker became an assistant surgeon for the army, and was awarded the Congressional Medal of Honor.

<u>Voluntary Groups</u>: Organizations helped to meet special needs of soldiers. The U.S. Sanitary Commission raised money through "Sanitary Fairs": a program to supply food, clothing, bandages, and medicine for the troops. The YMCA and Protestant ministers formed the Christian Commission to provide nursing care, blankets, and medicine to wounded soldiers. The Catholic Sisters of Charity supplied nurses to army hospitals.

Activity: Recalling Information (p. 55)
(Answers will vary but may include:)

1. The suspension of the writ of *habeas corpus* gave the military the right to arrest, imprison, and hold civilians without a trial.
2. The War Department made a policy that religious objectors were to be used in hospitals, they could take care of freedmen, or pay $300 for the care of sick and wounded soldiers.
3. If a newspaper was believed to be disloyal, the army might arrest the editor and hold him for a few days or refuse to allow papers to be mailed.
4. The court decided that the president could not try civilians in military courts in areas where regular courts were already operating.

Activity: Recalling Information (p. 57)
<u>Purpose of the War</u>
President Lincoln: save the Union
Congress: save the Union
<u>Freeing Slaves</u>
President Lincoln: Border States should free slaves
Leaders of the Border States: did not want slavery to end
<u>Black Soldiers</u>
President Lincoln: opposed the idea of enlisting black soldiers at first; by early 1863, favored the enlistment of black men into the army
Frederick Douglass: wanted black men to be able to serve in the Union Army

Activity: Making Inferences (p. 59)
(Answers will vary but may include:)

1. General Lee's Confederate Army gained confidence from their victory at Fredericksburg in 1862. Also, the Union Army had acquired a defeatist spirit after their crushing defeat.
2. General Hooker was a boastful man. His boasting bothered Lincoln, who felt that defeating the enemy in battle was more important than capturing the Confederate's capital. After Lincoln appointed Hooker as commander, he warned him not to act rashly. This implies that Lincoln felt Hooker was someone who acted without thinking things through and needed to be warned.

Activity: Timeline (p. 61)
December 6, 1862: Grant begins efforts to find a way to bypass Confederate guns controlling the Mississippi River.
April 16, 1863: The Confederate guns on the bluffs of Vicksburg fire at Union troops trying to cross the Mississippi River.
May 25, 1863: General Grant's troops besiege the city of Vicksburg.
July 4, 1863: Confederate General Pemberton surrenders Vicksburg to General Grant.

Activity: Skim and Scan (p. 63)
<u>Union Generals</u>: Grant, Hooker, Milroy, Meade, Buford, Reynolds
<u>Confederate Generals</u>: Longstreet, Bragg, Lee, Jackson, Ewell, Hill, Stuart
<u>Statements</u>: 1. Hooker's, 2. cavalry, 3. Lee, 4. Confederate

Activity: Making Inferences (p. 65)
(Answers will vary but may include:)

<u>Day 1</u>: Lee ordered Ewell to follow and attack the fleeing Union Army. Ewell held back and did not attack. This provided the Union Army with a chance to regroup and take up defensive positions on the hill.
<u>Day 2</u>: Lee ordered Longstreet to attack, but Longstreet failed to get his troops in position in time to take advantage of the Union's weakness.
<u>Day 3</u>: Pickett's charge was made up of 10,500 Confederate soldiers formed in three ranks as if on parade. They moved forward at 110 paces a minute across a mile of open ground. This made them easy targets for the Union Army.

Activity: Citing Evidence (p. 67)

1. President Lincoln appointed Montgomery Meigs as quartermaster general of the U.S. Army to take charge of supplying the troops. He did "an excellent job of supplying the troops with clothing, shoes, and food."

2. Critics of Grant pointed to his "reputation for drinking, his poor grammar, and his inability to march in step."

3. When the war began, Sherman believed troops should follow the current rules: no stealing, robbery, or pillaging. A statement he made in 1864: "We are not only fighting hostile armies, but a hostile people, and must make old and young, rich and poor, feel the hard hand of war" shows his attitude had grown more harsh. Later, when the war was nearly won, his attitude changed again, and he "became more benevolent."

Activity: Summarizing (p. 69)
(Answers will vary but may include:)
<u>Battle of the Wilderness</u>: On May 4, 1864, General Grant and his army crossed the Rapidan River and moved into a region of Virginia (The Wilderness) covered with dense woods. General Longstreet, who pushed Union troops back from Lee's headquarters, was accidently shot by one of his own men. Brush fires broke out, and at times the battle stopped so the wounded could be rescued. Although Grant planed to destroy Lee here, there was no clear winner in the three-day battle.
<u>Battle at Spotsylvania</u>: The Union Army was heading south to Spotsylvania. General Richard Anderson (now commanding Longstreet's men) had dug five miles of trenches before the Yankees arrived. Shaped like the letter U, the trenches allowed Confederate troops to easily move from one position to another and meet Union advances head on. The weakest spot in the U became known as "Bloody Angle" because of the fierce fighting in this location. There was no clear winner in the Battle of Spotsylvania, and both sides sustained heavy causalities.
<u>Battle at Cold Harbor</u>: The Union cavalry seized the crossroads to Cold Harbor. Soon after the Confederate infantry arrived, the troops were in position and digging in. The attack began on June 3 and continued to June 12. In the end, the Confederate Army would score a victory, and Cold Harbor would be Grant's last "battle in the Wilderness."

Activity: Recalling Information (p. 71)
(Answers may vary but may include)
1. Critics felt Sherman exaggerated the number of Southern forces in Kentucky and they claimed he was insane.
2. Grant was promoted to general-in-chief. Since he could no longer actively lead the army in the West, he entrusted that job to his friend General William T. Sherman.
3. Joe Johnston was the first Confederate commander to oppose Sherman in his march to the Atlantic.
4. After taking Atlanta, Sherman burned the city. In "total warfare" they had to destroy all the supplies the Confederates might be able to use.

Activity: Key Details (p. 73)
(Answers will vary but may include:)
1. supported an opponent of Lincoln in the election of 1860; critical of Lincoln; ran the War Department effeciently
2. thought he should have been the Republican presidential candidate; made no secret of his opinion that he was smarter than Lincoln; offered to resign
3. felt he should have been the Republican presidential candidate; thought being secretary of state would make him the real power in government; offered to resign

Activity: Compare and Contrast (p.75)
<u>Political Party</u>
Lincoln: He was a Republican.
McClellan: He was a Democrat.
<u>Problems for the Candidate</u>
Lincoln: Critics blamed every military blunder that was made during the war on Lincoln. Senator Samuel Pomeroy of Kansas issued the Pomeroy Circular, urging that Lincoln be dropped from the ticket. Some Republicans wanted General John C. Fremont as a candidate.
McClellan: Democratic delegates were split between supporters and opponents of the war. The party platform called for both continuing the war and for peace. McClellan, a general twice removed of his duties by Lincoln, tried to separate himself from the Peace Democrats, but Republicans would not let the Democratic platform of continuing the war while striving for peace die as an issue.
<u>Election Outcome</u>
Lincoln: Lincoln won the election with 212 electoral votes.
McClellan: McClellan only received 12 electoral votes.

Activity: Cause and Effect (p. 77)
1. There was rioting and looting in Richmond, the Confederate capital.
2. The Confederacy seized federal assets, borrowed money, sold bonds, and printed money.
3. In some parts of the South, there were no sheriffs or police to arrest the criminals and no judges to hear their cases. Deserters gathered in the mountains, swamps, and remote areas and literally took over. Sometimes the Confederate Army was sent after them, but that took men away from the fighting.
4. About 175,000 to 200,000 Southerners were refugees for an extended period of time. Usually they drifted from city to city or tried to find a family member who would take them in.

Activity: Timeline (p. 79)

May 16, 1864: Union General Butler attempts to capture the Fort at Drewry's Bluff.

June 11, 1864: Union troops damage the railroad leading to Richmond at the battle of Trevilian Station.

July 12, 1864: Confederate troops attack Fort Stevens but are pushed back.

July 30, 1864: Union failure at Battle of the Crater

September 21, 1864: Battle of Fisher's Hill—Union victory

October 19, 1864: Battle of Cedar Creek—Confederate victory

Activity: Summarizing (p. 81)

1. Union Army
2. Confederate Army
3. On April 9, 1865, General Lee and his Confederate troops surrendered to General Grant at Wilmer McLean's house in the town of Appomattox Courthouse. Lee wore a dress uniform; Grant, coming off the battlefield, wore a dirty coat and mud-covered boots. The terms of the surrender were to parole Confederate troops, give them rations, and allow the defeated troops to take their horses and mules home with them.

Activity: Recalling Information (p. 83)

President Lincoln: The Confederacy underestimated Lincoln.

Blockade: The Confederacy failed to bring in more arms, gunpowder, medicine, and other vital items in the early days of the blockade that they would need later.

King Cotton Diplomacy: The Confederacy assumed that if England and France were cut off from Southern cotton, they would be forced to recognize and support Southern independence.

Taxes: Not collecting taxes resulted in the government not having a revenue source to support war efforts.

Slaves: The South thought slaves would help them win the war. However, slaves were not allowed to serve in the Confederate Army until a month before the war ended.

Activity: Recalling Information (p. 85)

1. Booth planned to hold President Lincoln hostage until Southern prisoners of war were released.
2. The fall of Richmond and General Lee's surrender to General Grant at Appomattox Courthouse on April 9 caused Booth to change his plan.
3. Booth wanted to throw the Union government into chaos, allowing the South to reorganize.
4. George Atzerodt was to kill Vice President Johnson. Lewis Powell was to kill Secretary of State Seward.

Activity: Event and Impact (p. 87)

(Answers will vary but may include:)

Slavery: The war ended slavery, which led to the passage of the 13th Amendment.

The South: The Civil War caused billions of dollars of damage to the South. Towns and cities, large plantations, small farms, roads, bridges, and railroads were left in ruins. The destruction caused by the war forced the South to begin a rebuilding process. This era of Reconstruction would be filled with bribery and corruption.

The North: War brought about change to industries. Large factories replaced small shops, and businesses went from selling to local markets to national markets. Small farms could not compete with large farms that could afford new equipment.

Westward Expansion: During the war, Congress passed the Homestead and Pacific Railroad Acts. After the war, former soldiers moved to the west. Goods and people could travel from the Atlantic to the Pacific faster and easier thanks to the new railroads.